THEIR
LAST SUPPERS

THEIR LAST SUPPERS

Legends of History and Their Final Meals

Andrew Caldwell

Andrews McMeel
Publishing, LLC

Kansas City · Sydney · London

ISBN-13: 978-0-7407-9783-5
ISBN-10: 0-7407-9783-2

Library of Congress Control Number: 2009943929

10 11 12 13 14 RR4 10 9 8 7 6 5 4 3 2 1

www.andrewsmcmeel.com

ATTENTION: SCHOOLS AND BUSINESSES
Andrews McMeel books are available at quantity discounts with bulk purchase for educational, business, or sales promotional use. For information, please write to: Special Sales Department, Andrews McMeel Publishing, LLC, 1130 Walnut Street, Kansas City, Missouri 64106.

For my lovely daughters,
Juanita, Sheridan, and Celeste

Contents

Foreword xi

Handy Hints and Tips xiii

Captain Edward John Smith   **1**
RMS *Titanic*, North Atlantic
April 15, 1912

Martin Luther King   **13**
Memphis, Tennessee
April 4, 1968

Napoleon Bonaparte   **21**
Defeated at Waterloo, Belgium
June 18, 1815

Alexander the Great   **33**
Babylon, Iraq
June 13, 323 B.C.

Diana, Princess of Wales   **45**
Paris, France
August 30, 1997

John F. Kennedy   **53**
Dallas, Texas
November 22, 1963

Montezuma II, Last Aztec Emperor   **63**
Tenochtitlan
June 30, 1520

Rasputin   73
St. Petersburg, Russia
December 20, 1916

Cleopatra   85
Alexandria, Egypt
August 6, 30 B.C.

Admiral Horatio Nelson   93
HMS *Victory*, Trafalgar, Spain
October 21, 1805

Abraham Lincoln   103
Washington, D.C.
April 14, 1865

Leonidas, King of Sparta   111
Thermopylae, Greece
August 18, 480 B.C.

Captain Ernst Lehmann   119
The *Hindenburg*, Lakehurst, New Jersey
May 6, 1937

Elvis Aaron Presley   131
Graceland, Memphis, Tennessee
August 16, 1977

Lord Frederick Chelmsford   141
Defeated at Isandlwana, South Africa
January 22, 1879

Gaius Julius Caesar   151
The Curia, Rome
March 15, 44 B.C.

George Armstrong Custer   161
Little Bighorn
June 25, 1876

Adolf Hitler   169
The Führerbunker, Berlin, Germany
April 30, 1945

Marilyn Monroe   179
Brentwood, California
August 5, 1962

Captain James Cook   191
Kealakekua Bay, Hawaii
February 14, 1779

John Franklin Candy   201
Durango, Mexico
March 4, 1994

Foreword

Since my early childhood I have been fascinated by all types of history, and over the years I have been fortunate to visit the pyramids of Egypt and Mexico, Roman ruins in England, France, and Spain, the conquistador trails of the New World, and the pirate haunts of the Caribbean. I was trained as a head chef and resort manager in some of the world's finest resorts at the same time, enabling me to pursue my interests even more.

Eventually I was able to own my own little hotel in Albuquerque, New Mexico, where I was able to combine my love of food and history, for the enjoyment of our guests. Cocktail parties to celebrate the likes of Attila the Hun and Davy Crockett became themed weekends and a vital part of our business. I was struck by how little people seemed to know about historical events and how interested they became when an opportunity to discuss them came up. And so the idea for *Their Last Suppers* was born.

It's an effort to combine tales of the past with interesting menu ideas. All the principals here died untimely deaths that shook the world of their time, except for two: Napoleon lost only an empire at the Battle of Waterloo, and Lord Chelmsford mightily embarrassed one at the hands of the Zulus in South Africa. These were all powerful people in the prime of life, and their meals reflect the best of a varied and interesting choice of recipes, which help provide an insight into two thousand years of culinary history.

In doing my research for this book I noticed that nearly all these people made curious decisions that ultimately helped bring about their downfall. General Custer declined a Gatling gun battery en route to Little Bighorn on the grounds that it would slow him down. After a hectic day of travel, Princess Diana elected to leave the luxury of the Imperial Suite at the Ritz Hotel in Paris at midnight and drive to other lodgings across town. Captain Smith, of *Titanic* fame, was actually accelerating the ship toward known ice fields. President Kennedy's staff took the bulletproof top off his limousine so that he could enjoy the weather in Dallas.

Although it has been possible to discover the exact last meal eaten by many of the people here, in a couple of cases such as Alexander the Great, accustomed to four- and five-day banquets, the best I have been able to do is select a few royal dishes of his time.

Likewise, although the kitchens of Montezuma, Caesar, and the rest were usually very basic affairs consisting of no more than spits, clay baking ovens, and open fires, I have attempted to bring the foods into modern kitchens with all our advantages and cooking aids, although I believe that wherever possible, grills and open fires should be used for these dishes.

For the sake of healthful eating, I suggest the use of extra virgin olive oil with most recipes, and for the same reason I have cut down on the salt content of most ancient foods.

I leave the appropriate drinks to the reader's taste because the Mexican beers of today are a lot more palatable than the green lake water foam the Aztecs considered a delicacy, and the modern gourmand may not appreciate the pork blood beverage of the hardy Spartans.

HANDY HINTS AND TIPS

Grilling

Many of the ancient recipes in the book can be prepared on a regular barbecue to gain the same effect as an open fire. There are some basic techniques to be aware of when cooking on a grill:

- Light the fire with rolled-up newspapers and a little kindling before adding the coals to it.

- Do not use lighter fluid, because it adds a greasy taste to food.

- Try to anticipate how long you want to use the barbecue. Remember, most coals need to burn for at least 30 minutes to get the even temperature needed for cooking.

- Most coals burn for 45 to 60 minutes. For longer-cooking dishes (e.g., turkey), add more coals on a regular basis.

- For large items, place a drip tray on top of the coals; this will collect fats and juices to make a nice sauce and prevent flare-ups that damage the meat.

- Don't be afraid to experiment with wood. Most fruit trees and herbs provide good smoky flavors, along with the staples of oak, maple, and hickory. Soak woods for 30 minutes to bring out the maximum flavor.

- Cook small items, such as chops, poultry pieces, and seafood, with an open top; this increases the heat and seals the juices in quickly.

- For larger items, such as whole chickens, racks of ribs, or lamb, cover the grill; this makes the air inside the barbecue circulate and cooks the food evenly.

- Don't throw away unburnt wood and coals when you've finished cooking your meal. Wash off old materials and mix with new ones when grilling again.

- Always be aware of what has been on the grill. Keep fish, poultry, and meats in their own places and clean the grill thoroughly with a wire brush before allowing new foods to be put on it.

- For barbecue dishes use colored plates and fresh herbs for decoration. Keep the presentation simple.

- Everything can be grilled: Fish, poultry, meats, and vegetables all absorb the wonderful smell and feel of the open air. The key is to pay attention; in time you will feel comfortable assembling whole meals, even soups, on the grill, and will love the flavors and simplicity of your dishes.

Marinades

The simpler the better. To re-create foods and flavors of the past, olive oil, rosemary, sea salt, and black pepper with garlic and lemon juice do it every time.

The recipes of ancient Greece and Rome were often very basic dishes. Stuffed ostriches, bear claws, and pickled thrush tongues were always served for special occasions, but the heart of those cultures was built around simple grilled dishes, easy to prepare, easy to cook, easy on the eye.

Lemon Herb Marinade

This basic marinade recipe can be used for 8 pieces of chicken, fish, or chops.

    10 finely chopped garlic cloves
    juice of 4 fresh lemons
    sea salt and ground black pepper
    4 oz extra virgin olive oil
    3 tbsp freshly chopped rosemary

- Combine all ingredients.
- For best results, leave in the fridge overnight, but always marinate for at least 2 hours.

Basic Wine Marinade

This recipe can be used for 2 lb of game, beef, lamb, or fish. You can use red wine marinade for chicken or white wine marinade for lamb; they both work.

    4 tbsp red or white wine
    4 tbsp extra virgin olive oil
    2 finely chopped garlic cloves
    1½ tsp chopped fresh herbs
    sea salt and ground black pepper to taste

- Combine the ingredients.
- Marinate the fish for at least 30 minutes, fowl for 1 hour, red meat for at least 2 hours.

Tip: After removing marinated dishes from the fridge, always allow them to come to room temperature before cooking, and always brush off excess marinade.

Flavored Butters

For an exciting accompaniment to your roasts, grills, and fish dishes, there is an easy recipe: butter! Use any flavor. There are no hidden recipes; just soften your favorite butter and add your favorite ingredients in the quantity you like, roll in foil, then refrigerate. Here are some ideas:

Coriander and green chili butter
Rosemary–mustard butter
Green and black peppercorn butter
Mango and roasted garlic butter
Lime and rosemary butter
Black olive and sage butter
Red chili and parsley butter

Flavored Oils

Likewise, take your favorite olive oil, add whatever ingredients you like, and seal with a cork; it will keep for more than a year and add tremendous flavor to your cooking. Examples:

Spring onion oil
Thyme and rosemary oil
Garlic oil
Sage and garlic oil
Red chili oil

CAPTAIN EDWARD JOHN SMITH
RMS *Titanic*, North Atlantic
April 15, 1912

It gives me the greatest pleasure to captain this
most magnificent and unsinkable ship.

—Captain Smith, 1912

Nearly swamping a French trawler, the White Star Lines flagship RMS *Titanic* pulled away from its last ever contact with land at Queenstown in Ireland on the afternoon of April 11, 1912.

The eagerly awaited maiden voyage of the most luxurious and biggest liner ever built carried more than 1,200 of America's and Europe's wealthiest citizens, along with some 900 crew. And it was captained by the world's best-paid seaman, the Commodore of the White Star Line, Edward John Smith. It was, ironically, his last scheduled voyage.

E.J., as everyone in the Merchant Navy knew him, was born in Hanley, England, in 1850. On leaving school at the age of 13 he went to Liverpool to begin an apprenticeship under sail, eventually joining the famous White Star Line in 1880, moving quickly through its ranks to his first naval command in 1887.

Within 2 years he had the first of many accidents, running the *Republic* aground in New York Harbor. Then, when it was finally refloated and reached the port, a furnace exploded in the engine room, killing three crewmen and seriously wounding seven others. The unflappable captain reported to the ship's owners that they had had a "minor incident." In 1890, he introduced the *Coptic* to the sandbanks outside the harbor of Rio de Janeiro. A series of other "minor incidents" occurred over the following decade, and in 1901, while in charge of the *Majestic*, he once again experienced a major fire on board in a linen closet and several cabins. By ripping up the deck and blasting in steam the crew avoided a real tragedy, but in the ensuing inquiry Smith calmly testified that no one had even informed him of any fire on board.

In 1906, while Smith was on the *Baltic*, moored in Liverpool, another large fire mysteriously broke out, taking some 640 bales of wood and other cargo but fortunately no lives. In 1907, approaching New York Harbor once again, this time on the *Adriatic*, Smith ran aground once again, this time at the entrance of Ambrose Channel.

On the *Olympic*'s maiden voyage to New York in 1911, he trapped and almost crushed a tug on June 21, collided with the warship HMS Hawk on September 20, and ran over a submerged wreck on February 24, 1912, losing a propeller in the process.

When interviewed by the *New York Times* in 1907 about his troubles at sea, the captain cheerfully replied, "None really, apart from bad weather." For all his mishaps he was admired by both owners and crew and was given a £200 no-collision bonus every year.

Second officer Charles Lightoller, who survived the *Titanic* disaster, spoke fondly of the skipper at the inquiry. "It was an education to see him con his ship up through the intricate channels, entering New York harbor at full speed. . . . One particularly bad corner . . . used to make us flush with pride as he swung her around, judging his distance to a nicety, she heeling over to the helm with only a few feet to spare between each end of the ships and the banks."

This was the man placed in charge of the company flagship. And as Smith gave a brief whistle of apology to the French trawler that bright sunny afternoon in Ireland, the *Titanic* was already speeding toward an area of the North Atlantic ocean known to be infested with far more ice fields than normal because of an unusually mild winter in Greenland.

In keeping with Smith's tradition of "not hanging around," the *Titanic* covered 464 miles on its first day and 519 the next, then 546 from the next Saturday to Sunday at noon. Each day brought even more acceleration, and on the day before the sinking he was planning more speed trials, although he knew that heavy ice was dead ahead.

The *Titanic* was more than 882 feet long and displaced some 66,000 tons. It represented the best of everything of its day. Dozens of chefs prepared huge multicourse meals, based on the cuisine of Auguste Escoffier. And hundreds of stewards attended every whim of its passengers. There were Turkish baths, a swimming pool, a gymnasium, squash courts, and all manner of entertainments for its pampered guests.

For all its refinements, the *Titanic* had only enough lifeboats for about half the passengers, because it was considered totally unsinkable. Another minor oversight, particularly because they were heading toward heavy ice, was that the main lookout system for the ship, the crow's nest, had been given no binoculars.

Early on the morning of Sunday, April 14, the *Titanic*, moving at close to top speed, received the first of many warnings about ice ahead from the *Caronia*. At 9 A.M. yet another message from one of the captain's former commands, the *Baltic*, specifically warned, "Heavy ice directly on your course." Unperturbed, the captain went about his normal routine, having an early breakfast in his cabin and then touring the ship with his officers, before retiring to prepare for dinner that evening in the à la carte restaurant with wealthy American bankers Mr. and Mrs. George Widener of Philadelphia.

After a leisurely dinner with his guests, the captain excused himself at 9 P.M. and had a brief chat with the officer of the watch before retiring to his bed at 9:30 P.M.

Events began to unfold rapidly. High above the speeding ship, in the freezing cold of the crow's nest, the two lookouts, Fred Fleet and Reginald Lee, stared ahead as the *Titanic*, still at full speed, moved serenely over a flat ocean. The outside air was freezing at

0°C, and the water temperature suddenly dropped a half a degree below that (salt water freezes at a lower temperature than fresh water), an ominous sign.

The wireless room became even busier as reports of heavy ice began to flood in from other ships and the distant coastline. Incredibly, at 10:30 P.M. the bridge received a message by signal lamp from SS *Rappahannock*, a cargo ship passing just a few miles to the north: "Have just passed through heavy ice and icebergs." The bridge replied, "Message received, thank you and goodnight," but no one thought to disturb the captain or attempt to slow the ship.

Thirty minutes later the *Californian*, which was just ahead, warned that it was jammed by ice, to which they got the reply, "Keep out, shut up, you're jamming our signals" from the now overloaded wireless room.

At 11:30 P.M., only half an hour before the end of their shift, the anxious lookouts noticed a low-lying area of mist ahead, and the cold air around them suddenly became very damp, adding to their discomfort even more. Complete silence enveloped them as they strained to penetrate the mist with their eyes. Then Fleet gave three desperate tugs on the crow's nest bell and screamed over the telephone to the bridge officer, James Moody Toft, some 70 feet below, "Iceberg right ahead!"

Some 40 seconds after this warning, as the crew strained every sinew to change direction, the RMS *Titanic*, traveling at 22.5 knots, struck a large iceberg in what seemed a glancing blow.

Though only lasting about 10 seconds, the contact was enough to rip open a gash more than 300 feet long down the ship's flank, and although it was only a few inches wide, it was a mortal blow. The "unsinkable" *Titanic*, the greatest ship ever built, had a little less than 3 hours left.

Within the first hour Captain Smith knew his ship was doomed, and he immediately ordered the lifeboats to be lowered and filled with women and children. In the inquest after the disaster survivors told harrowing stories of how landed English gentlemen retired with their valets to their cabins "to dress appropriately." Others tried to dress as women to get on the lifeboats.

The eight-piece band, under conductor Wallace Hartley, remained on board playing ragtime music in a futile attempt to cheer people up as the ship slowly started to tilt under them. At 2:20 A.M. the lights began to flicker for the last time, and the band, knowing this would be their final song, elected to finish with the hymn "Nearer My God to Thee." They then accompanied Captain Smith and 1,500 other passengers and crew to their deaths in the freezing waters, as the *Titanic* slid over two and a half miles downward to its final resting place on the sea bottom, where it lay undisturbed for decades.

LAST MENU ON THE *TITANIC*
Meals in Edwardian times often went on for 3 or 4 hours.

1st Course: Hors d'Oeuvres

Hors d'Oeuvres

Oysters à la Russe

2nd Course: Soups

Consommé Olga

Cream of Barley

3rd Course: Fish

Poached Salmon

Mousseline Sauce

4th Course: Entrées

Filet Mignon Lili

Chicken Lyonnaise

Vegetable Marrow Farci

5th Course: Removes

Lamb with Mint Sauce

Calvados Glazed Roast Duck with Apple Sauce

Roast Sirloin of Beef Forestière

Chateau Potatoes, Minted Green Pea Timbales, Creamed Carrots,
Boiled Rice Parmentier, Boiled New Potatoes

6th Course: Sorbet or Punch

Punch Romaine

7th Course: Roast

Roasted Squab on Wilted Cress

8th Course: Salad

Asparagus Salad with Champagne–Saffron Vinaigrette

9th Course: Cold Dish

Pâté de Foie Gras

Celery

10th Course: Sweets

Waldorf Pudding

Peaches in Chantreuse Jelly

Chocolate-Painted Éclairs

French Vanilla Ice Cream

11th Course: Dessert

Assorted Fresh Fruits and Cheeses

After Dinner

Coffee

Cigars

CAPTAIN SMITH'S LAST MEAL

While on board the *Titanic*, Captain Smith ate in the elegant first-class dining saloon, where he had his own table for six. For his last meal of April 14, 1912, he was a guest of an American couple in the à la carte dining room, known as the Ritz because of its imitation of the Ritz Carlton restaurants inspired by Auguste Escoffier. The *Titanic* had huge refrigeration and storage facilities, and had stocked its fridges with even more luxury items for this maiden voyage. The captain had a light meal that night.

Oysters à la Russe (1)

Particularly popular with the gentry of the age, this is an excellent dish, easy to prepare and perfectly accompanied by a crisp Chablis or white burgundy.

12 large oysters, well cleaned under running water
2 large shots Russian vodka
juice of one lemon
½ tsp fresh creamed horseradish
dash of Tabasco
pinch sea salt
1 large tomato, blanched, seeded, and chopped

- Remove top halves of oysters, separate membranes from lower shells, and place on crushed ice.
- Combine all other ingredients.
- Spoon mix onto oysters, sprinkle with crushed black pepper, and enjoy!

Filet Mignon Lili with Pommes Anna (4)

4 fillet steaks, cut from the center of the fillet, approximately
    2 inches thick, 8 oz each (Angus steak or corn-fed beef is
    preferable)
4 slices bacon
4 oz unsalted butter
4 tsp extra virgin olive oil
ground sea salt and black pepper to taste
2 cups French red wine
16 canned artichoke hearts (cut in quarters)
6 large garlic cloves, peeled and thinly sliced

- Wrap the bacon slices around the steaks and secure with wooden cocktail sticks.
- Heat the oil and butter in a frying pan until just below smoking. Put in steaks, turning every few seconds until brown on all sides. Cook for no more than 4 minutes, then remove steaks from pan.
- Add garlic to pan, remove the bacon, and seal sides of steaks for about 1 minute; remove the steaks and place on the Pommes Anna.
- Deglaze the pan with red wine, add the artichoke hearts for about 2 minutes, and spoon over the steaks and potatoes.

Pommes Anna (4)

3 cups unsalted melted butter
12 large baking potatoes, peeled and thinly sliced
salt and pepper to taste

- Brush a 2-inch-deep ovenproof skillet with butter and lay overlapping slices of potato with light seasoning, brush with butter, and build layers.
- Cook for 8 to 10 minutes on open stove.
- Cover with foil; place in oven for 15 to 20 minutes at 450°F.
- Cut the potatoes into wedges and serve with the Filet Mignon Lili.

Calvados Glazed Duckling with Apple Sauce (4)

2 large ducklings, preferably wild, about 9–11 lb each
4 cloves chopped garlic
1 large chopped red onion
1 cup chopped celery
½ cup chopped parsley
12 oz clear beef stock (or canned consommé)
3 tsp Worcestershire sauce
salt and pepper to taste
4 cups Calvados (an apple liqueur from Normandy)

- Rub the duckling inside and out with a little salt and pepper and rub the outside with Worcestershire sauce.
- Combine all other ingredients (except the Calvados and consommé) and stuff the mixture loosely into the ducks.
- Place the ducks (breast side down) in a hot roasting tray and cook for 20 minutes, then pour on the Calvados and consommé.
- Roast for about 3 hours at 325 to 350°F, basting every 15 minutes.
- Turn the ducks over and roast for another 30 to 40 minutes until golden, basting as often as possible.
- Serve hot on a bed of watercress with apple sauce.

Apple Sauce (4)

4 lb cooking apples
4 oz butter
10 tbsp sugar

- Peel, core, and quarter the apples, then slice and place in a pan with about 10 tbsp water; cover and cook gently for about 8 minutes until soft.
- Purée in a blender, add butter, and sweeten to taste.

Fresh Asparagus Salad
with Champagne–Saffron Vinaigrette (4)

2 lb fresh asparagus
2 oz Dijon mustard
1 glass Dom Perignon
2 oz olive oil
½ tsp fresh saffron
salt and pepper to taste

- The classic test of where to cut asparagus is to bend it gently. At the point it is ready to crack, cut it there, and discard the hard stems.
- Place the asparagus tips in boiling salted water for 4 minutes, remove, strain off the hot water, and place the asparagus in ice water (this keeps it green and fresh).
- For the dressing, combine the chopped saffron, salt, pepper, and mustard into a base, gently whisk in the oil and champagne in equal amounts, pour on chilled asparagus, and serve.
- Serve with a cold burgundy, champagne, or cold sparkling wine.

MARTIN LUTHER KING
Memphis, Tennessee
April 4, 1968

Well, I don't know what will happen now, we've got some
difficult days ahead, but it really doesn't matter with me
now because I have been to the mountain top.

—Martin Luther King, Memphis, April 3, 1968

U.S. Baptist minister and civil rights leader Martin Luther King was a man of extraordinary vision. In a time of intense segregation in America, King inspired the black people of the United States to walk in the footsteps of Gandhi and try to obtain justice by peaceful protest and nonviolent direct action. He was gunned down by James Earl Ray on April 4. His life can be summed up no better than by the vibrant speech he made to the crowds at the Lincoln Memorial in Washington, D.C., on August 28, 1963.

The government of his day demonized him; he was constantly followed by the FBI and other federal agencies and portrayed as a troublemaker or criminal working against America. He rose above the bigotry of the time to conduct himself with dignity and power at a time when the Ku Klux Klan was at its height and black children were denied education in the "Land of the Free." That he was vilified and hounded by the authorities and still came up with the following contribution is a fitting tribute to his spirit.

I am happy to join with you today in what will go down in history as the greatest demonstration of freedom in the history of our nation.

Five score years ago, a great American, in whose symbolic shadow we stand today, signed the Emancipation Proclamation. This momentous decree came as a great beacon light of hope to millions of Negro slaves who had been seared in the flames of withering injustice. It came as a joyous daybreak to end the long night of their captivity.

But, one hundred years later the Negro still is not free. One hundred years later the manacles of segregation and the chains of discrimination still sadly cripple the life of the Negro. One hundred years later the Negro lives on a lonely island of poverty in the midst of a vast ocean of material prosperity. One hundred years later the Negro is still languishing in the corners of American society and finds himself in exile in his own land.

So we've come here today to dramatize a shameful condition. In a sense, we've come to our nation's capital to cash a check. When the architects of our republic wrote the magnificent words of the Constitution and the Declaration of Independence, they were signing a promissory note to which every American was to fall heir. This note was a promise that all men—yes, black men as well as white men—would be guaranteed the inalienable rights of life, property, and the pursuit of happiness.

It is obvious today that America has defaulted on this promissory note insofar as her citizens of color are concerned. Instead of honoring this sacred obligation, America has given the Negro people a bad check which has come back marked "insufficient funds." But we refuse to believe that the bank of justice is bankrupt. There will be neither rest nor tranquility in America until the Negro is granted his citizenship rights. The whirlwind of revolt will continue to shake the foundations of our Nation until the bright day of justice emerges.

But there is something that I must say to my people who stand on the warm threshold, which leads into the palace of justice. In the process of gaining our rightful place, we must not be guilty of wrongful deeds. Let us not seek to satisfy our thirst for freedom by drinking from the cup of bitterness and hatred.

We must forever conduct our struggle on the high plane of dignity and discipline. We must not allow our creative protest to degenerate into physical violence. Again and again we must rise to the majestic heights of meeting physical force with soul force.

The marvelous new militancy which has engulfed the Negro community, must not lead us to a distrust of all white people, for many of our white brothers, as evidenced by their presence here today, have come to realize that their destiny is tied up with our destiny. . . .

So even though we face the difficulties of today and tomorrow, I still have a dream. It is a dream deeply rooted in the American dream. I have a dream that one day this nation will rise up and live out the true meaning of its creed. We hold these truths to be self-evident, that all men are created equal.

I have a dream that one day on the red hills of Georgia sons of former slaves and sons of former slave owners will be able to sit down together at the table of brotherhood. I have a dream. That one day—even the State of Mississippi, a state sweltering with the heat of injustice, sweltering with the heat of oppression—will be transformed into an oasis of freedom and justice. I have a dream. That my four little children will one day live in a nation where they will not be judged by the color of their skin but by the content of their character. I have a dream today.

I have a dream that one day down in Alabama, with its vicious racists, with its Governor having his lips dripping with the words of interposition and nullification, one day right there in Alabama, little black boys and black girls will be able to join hands with little white boys and white girls as sisters and brothers. I have a dream today. . . .

Let freedom ring, and when this happens—when we allow freedom to ring, when we let it ring from every village and every hamlet, from every state and every city we will be able to speed up that day when all of God's children— black men and white men, Jews and Gentiles, Protestants and Catholics—will be able to join hands and sing in the words of the old Negro spiritual: Free at last. Free at last. Thank God Almighty, we are free at last.

MENUS

Last Dinner

Southern Fried Chicken

Louisiana Hot Sauce and Vinegar

Black-Eyed Peas

Collard Greens

Cornbread

Favorite Food

Catfish Creole

Southern Fried Chicken (4)

1 frying chicken (remove skin if you want low fat), cut into 8
    pieces
3 tsp seasoned salt
2 finely chopped garlic cloves
1 cup all-purpose flour
1 cup vegetable oil

- Season the chicken with all the seasonings, roll the pieces in the
  flour until covered, shake off excess flour.
- Fry gently in oil until golden brown, turning frequently.

Tip: Start with the oil at a very high temperature, then reduce the
heat after a minute or two. This seals in the moisture and the flour,
and then helps cook it through.

Collard Greens

2 lb fresh green collards
1–2 gallons water
1 or 2 ham hocks
1 tbsp salt
2 dried red peppers
1 cup chopped onion

- In a large pot, boil the water with the ham hocks and salt; ham is very salty, so salt is optional.
- Clean and add the greens a few at a time along with the other ingredients. Cover and boil for about 1 hour. Serve immediately.

Cornbread

2–4 tbsp shortening or bacon drippings
1½ cups white self-rising cornmeal
½ cup all-purpose flour
1 egg
½ cup buttermilk or sweet milk
¼ tsp baking soda if using buttermilk
water

- Preheat oven to 425°F.
- Put the shortening in a cast iron skillet and place in the oven.
- Combine the cornmeal and flour, then mix in the egg and milk, add the water slowly until the mixture is like a thick pancake batter.
- Place mixture in skillet and bake 20 to 25 minutes in oven until golden brown.

Louisiana Hot Sauce and Vinegar

3 cups distilled white vinegar
2 tsp salt
2 lb seeded and chopped cayenne or jalapeño peppers

- Simmer the vinegar, salt, and peppers for at least 5 minutes.
- Blend the mix in a food processor.
- Store in glass bottles in a dark place for at least 3 months to bring out optimum flavor.
- Strain when ready to use; serve chilled or hot.

Black-Eyed Peas

1½ cups dried black-eyed peas
½ tsp garlic powder
1 tsp salt
½ tsp black pepper
2 tbsp olive oil
1 tbsp chopped onion
1 small piece salt pork

- Soak the peas overnight in enough water to cover them.
- Drain them, put in a pan, and then cover with about 2½ cups of hot water. Add the other ingredients, then simmer for about 1½ hours, or until the peas are soft.

Catfish Creole

1 lb catfish fillets
1 cup sliced celery
⅓ cup olive oil
1 chopped bell pepper, red or green
½ cup water
2 cloves crushed garlic
¼ cup flour
1 lb tomatoes chopped
1 tsp brown sugar
1½ tsp sea salt
1 tbsp lemon juice
2 bay leaves
¼ cup chopped parsley
½ tsp thyme
1 tsp Worcestershire sauce
2 dashes Tabasco sauce
2 cups hot cooked rice

- Cut the fish into 1- to 2-inch pieces. Heat the oil in a large flat pan; add the flour, stirring gently with a wooden spatula until brown. Remove from heat and slowly add water until thoroughly blended.
- Add all the other ingredients, except the catfish and rice. Cover the pot and simmer for about 20 minutes.
- Remove bay leaves, add the catfish, and simmer for another 8 to 10 minutes. Serve immediately over hot rice in soup bowls.

NAPOLEON BONAPARTE
Defeated at Waterloo, Belgium
June 18, 1815

Give me night, or give me Blücher.

—Duke of Wellington, Waterloo, June 18, 1815

Born in the humble town of Ajaccio in Corsica in 1769, Napoleon Bonaparte became one of the greatest adventurers the world had ever seen. Inspiring the people of France to follow him on a whirlwind trip to glory, he rode the wave of the French Revolution until his own overambition and the combined forces of Europe aligned to bring about his total defeat.

A short but extremely dynamic person, Napoleon was always questioning the old methods of warfare throughout his education at the military schools of Brienne and Paris. With the advent of the New Republic, his talents as an innovative and driven artillery officer in the French war with Italy heralded a spectacular rise to power. Adored and supported from the first by the army, he became First Consul of France on November 9, 1799, at the age of only 30, then attaining autocratic power for life only 3 years later, in 1802.

Wasting no time in consolidating power, he had himself declared emperor in 1804 in front of the Pope in Paris. This was a deliberate ploy to gain recognition of his authority, with a title that would expand the French borders. Simultaneously he combined a detailed reorganization of all aspects of French life with an almost constant succession of campaigns abroad, defeating the Austrians at the battle of Austerlitz (1805) and then Prussia at Jena (1806), finally threatening France's old enemy, Britain, with invasion and blockade.

He briefly formed a treaty with the Russians in 1807 at Tilsit, but this was a pact he had no intention of honoring. His boundless energy and military victories soon became the talk of Europe. He showed continued brilliance at the head of his armies, which eventually led him to a feeling of invincibility and greed. This arrogance culminated in a failed campaign in Spain and then a disastrous march into Russia, which led to his army's infamous retreat from Moscow in 1812, leaving tens of thousands of his troops frozen to death in the grip of the savage Russian winter.

The end finally came at the battle of Leipzig, when he was confronted by several nations united and intent on his destruction and the subjugation of France. They finally forced his abdication, and he was exiled to the island of Elba with only 1,000 of his loyal guardsmen to accompany him, in 1814. Europe celebrated, but not for long.

Within only a few months, desperate to regain his throne, he escaped from the island and returned to France. The army dispatched to arrest him refused to confront him, and once again they flocked behind his banner. Knowing this was his last chance and that he must produce a decisive victory over the Allied armies arraigned against him throughout Europe, he made a sudden thrust against the forces of Prussia and Britain on June 16. This quick move split the Allied armies under General Blücher and the famous British leader, the Duke of Wellington, a general he had no real regard for because of his aristocratic background.

Blücher's army was hammered back, and Napoleon, sensing the kill, dispatched General Groucher to follow the Prussians with some 30,000 of his precious troops. He gave the general specific instructions to prevent the Prussians from reuniting with the British at any cost. Napoleon intended to finally destroy Wellington in one decisive battle the next day.

Given the news of Napoleon's sudden move at a regimental dinner that night, Wellington moved with equal surety, directing his army to form up in a defensive position astride the road to Brussels, outside the Soignes Forest and just outside the little-known village of Waterloo.

Torrential rain throughout the night of June 17 did not stop Napoleon's eager army from marching into position, and the morning of June 18 found both forces confronting each other across a sea of mud. Napoleon's generals were very wary of the English lord, but Napoleon was totally dismissive of Wellington, regarding the outcome of the battle as a foregone conclusion. With superior numbers of men and artillery Napoleon intended to brush Wellington aside and then march on to Brussels, some 11 miles away, eventually forcing Europe to sue for peace.

However, the Duke of Wellington was a very able and proven general. He had been undefeated in battle and was always extremely meticulous and resolute. He had previously visited the fields of Waterloo some years before and had studied the layout as if anticipating that one day he would fight his last, greatest battle there.

Napoleon and his staff set up headquarters in a large farmhouse called Le Caillou, and though trying to rest, he was constantly disturbed by the arrival of messengers. So at 1 A.M. in driving rain, he mounted his famous horse, La Désirée, and went to reconnoiter the outposts with General Bertrand.

Returning to the farmhouse at 4 A.M., he was greeted by the news that the Prussians had been split into two columns, one supposedly heading toward Liège and the other retreating in disorder. Seeing everything going as planned, he retired to bed, leaving orders that the troops were to be ready to advance at 9 A.M. He was completely unaware that Groucher was not harassing the Prussian retreat, as he had been instructed, and that the Prussians were marching back toward him and the battlefield.

At 7 A.M. he rose and dressed in his favorite uniform as a general of the Guard Chasseurs. He joined his generals, Soult, Lobau, Reille, the Duke of Bassono, and his brother Jerôme for breakfast in the humble dining room of the farmhouse. The food, though in simple surrounds, was served on the imperial silver that always accompanied him. Napoleon was good humored but constantly dismissive of the English forces arraigned against him.

Although the French line extended nearly 5 miles, Napoleon's sole intent that morning was to throw a disguised feint, then attack the English center with all his forces and break them as he had broken so many other armies before.

Although the rain eventually stopped, the sodden fields would not permit him to move his artillery and attacking forces into position quickly enough, and a frustrated Napoleon was forced to delay his attack until 11:35 A.M., a 2-hour delay that eventually proved his undoing.

The feint was thrown by his brother Jerôme at a heavily defended farmhouse on the British side called Hougoumont, with the main attack launched at the British troops in view on the ridgeline by the heavy infantry and artillery at 1 P.M. Napoleon's devastating firepower began to inflict heavy casualties on the British infantry, who slowly began to pull back over the crest of the hill. Believing the British line to be broken, his second in command, General Ney, flung the French cavalry in reckless pursuit of the retreating infantry, without consulting Napoleon, who was elsewhere on the battlefield.

Swarming over the top of the hill, thousands of French lancers expecting a rout were stunned to find themselves confronted by volleys of fire from even more thousands of troops in well-organized defensive squares. The cunning Wellington had kept most of his force out of sight on the other side of the hill, thus luring the French cavalry to its decimation, followed by a panicked retreat.

Meanwhile, down in the valley Jerôme was throwing endless lines of troops to their deaths at the Hougoumont farmhouse, determined to take control of the situation for his brother. He did just that at about 4 P.M., though at huge cost to the precious French reserves. Napoleon, who was incandescent with rage on realizing the mistake Ney had made, resolved to smash Wellington once and for all and launched attack after attack at the British front lines, which finally began to crumble under the terrible onslaught.

Several miles away, General Groucher bristled at the suggestion from his second in command that he "should march to the sound of the distant guns," stressing that his orders were only to follow Blücher and the retreating Prussians.

Not only was Groucher depriving Napoleon of what would have been a decisive force in the main engagement, but by lying back too far behind the Prussians he was enabling the wily Blücher to lead his men back toward Wellington and the battlefield of Waterloo.

Despite the incompetence of his generals, the superior numbers and artillery of the French were gradually wearing down the British defensive forces. The French infantry almost forced through the battered Wellington at 6 P.M., causing Wellington to shout, "Give me night, or give me Blücher," as he knew another such attack would finish him.

By now both commanders could see an army marching to the battlefield in the distance. Were the uniforms the blue of Groucher or the black of Prussia? They both got the answer from eagle-eyed officers at the same time: They were Prussian black.

In desperation, Napoleon ordered his famed Old Guard forward in the hope of smashing Wellington quickly; then he hoped to regroup and deal with the Prussians later. The Old Guard had been with him from the beginning. Grizzled veterans from many campaigns, they usually heralded an imminent French victory, and once again they advanced to the beat of their bands with supreme confidence.

But not today. Faced with a withering fire from every gun at Wellington's disposal, the Old Guard broke and retreated. With Blücher arriving on the field and urging his troops to show no mercy, the battle was quickly over and a massacre ensued, ending Napoleon's 100-day reign. Fleeing the battlefield, he tried to go to the United States on July 3 before abdicating once again, this time being imprisoned for life on the distant Isle of St. Helena on August 8.

A brilliant general and tactician in his prime and conqueror of Europe and Egypt, Napoleon Bonaparte died a broken man before his time, of suspected lead poisoning, in his island prison on May 5, 1821, at the age of only 52.

MENUS

Even in Le Caillou farmhouse before the Battle of Waterloo, Napoleon enjoyed a grand breakfast, served on imperial silver, with his generals.

Menu

Liver and Bacon Chops

Sautéed Kidneys in Sherry

Shirred Eggs with Cream

Garlic Toast with Roast Tomatoes

Favorite Foods

Chicken Marengo

Chestnut Soup

After being introduced to it in Egypt, Napoleon swore that chestnut soup could cure anything.

Chestnut Soup (8)

2 lb fresh chestnuts or 4½ cups canned chestnuts
2 tbsp butter
3 ribs celery, strings removed
2 onions, peeled and cut in half
2 leeks, white part only
1 crushed garlic clove
7 cups chicken stock
½ cup heavy cream
salt and pepper to taste

- To shell and peel fresh chestnuts, make a cross in the head of the chestnut with a sharp knife, place in a pan, cover with water, and bring to a boil. Allow chestnuts to cool, then peel. If using canned chestnuts, omit this step.
- Thinly slice the celery, onions, and leeks. Melt the butter in a large pan and slowly add celery, onions, leeks, and garlic. Cook them until they become translucent.
- Add the peeled chestnuts to the dish and cook gently for another 5 minutes.
- Add the chicken stock, the cream, and the salt and pepper to taste, and cover, cooking over low heat for another 10 minutes. Sprinkle with nutmeg. Serve hot or cold.

Chicken Marengo

The battle of Marengo over the Austrians, in June 1800, set the stage for this dish. His chef, Dunond, scoured the battlefield after the victory and came up with a few meager local ingredients that he gallantly threw together for his emperor, and it later became Napoleon's favorite dish; he ate it after every battle.

1 chicken cut into 8 pieces
1 tsp salt
1 dash pepper
4 tbsp olive oil
1 chopped onion
½ clove minced garlic
½ cup chopped tomatoes
½ cup sliced white truffle, optional
⅓ cup cognac or sherry
2 tbsp flour
6 eggs for garnishing

- Cut the chicken into pieces, sprinkle with salt, pepper, and flour, then brown in hot oil. Set aside.
- Sauté the onions and garlic in the same pan. Then add the chicken and the rest of the ingredients except eggs. Cover and simmer until tender, 30 to 40 minutes.
- Fry the eggs and place one on each dish as a garnish.
- Dunond also added a fried crayfish on each plate—great battle-field scavenging.

Calves' Liver (2)

4 thin slices calves' liver, about ¾ lb
salt and pepper
¼ cup flour
2 tbsp vegetable oil
3 tbsp butter
1 tbsp shallots, finely chopped
½ tbsp red wine vinegar
1 tbsp chopped parsley
1 tbsp chopped chives
½ tbsp chopped tarragon

- Place the liver, salt, pepper, and flour in a plastic bag to coat the liver and shake off the excess.
- Heat the oil in a frying pan and cook the liver about 1 minute per side until nicely browned.
- Remove the liver to a warm platter.
- Wipe out the pan with a clean cloth. Add the butter and cook over a high heat until the butter is a hazelnut brown color. Add the shallots, stir and cook for about 1 minute, then add the vinegar.
- Pour the hot sauce over the liver.
- Sprinkle with parsley, chives, and fresh tarragon; serve immediately.

Rognons de Veau Ardennaise (Veal Kidneys)

Accompanied by 2 cups hot cooked rice mixed with ¼ cup chopped parsley.

6 veal kidneys, split and cut into ½-inch slices
¼ cup butter
2 tbsp minced shallots
½ cup sliced mushrooms
2–3 tbsp diced green pepper
¼ cup brandy
⅓ cup chicken broth
1½ tbsp flour
salt and pepper to taste

- Sauté the shallots, mushrooms, and green peppers in the butter for about 5 minutes.
- Add the kidneys and simmer for another 5 minutes, stirring once or twice.
- Heat the brandy in a small saucepan. Light it and then pour over the kidneys and vegetables.
- When the flame dies, stir in the chicken broth, cover, turn heat to low, and cook for another 10 minutes.
- Mix the flour with the salt, pepper, and 3 tbsp water. Combine this with the kidney mixture and cook until it thickens, stirring constantly. Sprinkle with chopped parsley and serve.

Shirred Eggs

- Melt 2 oz butter in frying pan, add two fresh eggs, cook quickly, flip eggs.
- Serve with a spoonful of thick cream on top and chopped parsley.

Garlic Toast

2 loaves French bread
4–6 cloves garlic, halved

- Slice the bread lengthwise, then in serving-size pieces.
- Bake at 350°F for about 10 minutes.
- Lightly rub garlic cloves on both sides until it melts on the toast. Serve immediately.

ALEXANDER THE GREAT
Babylon, Iraq
June 13, 323 B.C.

Only sex and sleep make me conscious that I am mortal.

—Alexander

Alexander the Great, a name that has inspired generals and common people alike for more than 2,000 years, was born the son of King Phillip and Queen Olympias of Macedonia. The family was a highly militaristic one, and from an early age Alexander was bred for war and the expansion of Macedonian power.

Tutored as a child in the arts by the great Greek philosopher Aristotle but groomed even harder in military matters by his harsh father, Phillip, Alexander itched for conquest from his youth. Born in the town of Pella, some 50 miles from Thessalonica, the capital of ancient Macedonia, Alexander was brought up by his father and his equally manipulative mother with a vision to incorporate the states of the Greek world with their own dominant Macedonian army. This force could then be used primarily against their hereditary enemy, Persia, and would supposedly avenge all the wrongs done to the country in generations before by the despotic kings of the Asian Empire. More importantly, it would expand the aggressive Macedonian Empire.

While fighting at the side of his father against the forces of Thebes and Athens at the battle of Chae Ronea in 338 B.C., Alexander resolved to incorporate the fragmented Greek states into one united force when he had the chance. For many decades the Greeks had always divided their strength by fighting among themselves; in fact, a constant state of war existed between most Greek cities.

The opportunity he wanted arrived sooner than expected. Phillip's wife Olympias was always trying to position her offspring to succeed the ailing king and was constantly plotting his downfall. So it came as little surprise that when attending a local religious ceremony on foot, Phillip was stabbed to death in the streets of his own capital. A furious Alexander, though still a teenager, quickly took control of the army, and anybody he perceived as being unfaithful to him was put to death, including several of his own family. The handsome, eloquent Alexander was immediately revered by the Macedonian troops, especially when he outlined his vision for conquest and spoke to them of the glories and riches to come.

Constantly modeling himself on Homeric heroes such as his ancestor Achilles, Alexander demanded that the Greek states join him in a war against Persia or be destroyed by the new forces he was assembling. There would be no more squabbling between them. They would either join him or perish.

Light, fast-moving cavalry, impeccably drilled and supported by a dense mass of heavily armored infantry equipped with long pikes, called a phalanx, were the cornerstones of his new army. Moving quickly and attacking when least expected, the Macedonian-based troops quickly became an irresistible force. The Greeks had no choice but to acquiesce, and so in 334 B.C., with about 32,000 infantry, 5,000 horses, and 160 ships, Alexander crossed the Hellespont waterway into Asia.

Standing on the prow of the first galley, he threw a spear into the approaching beach, shouting, "I now declare all this land to be mine by right of spear!"

Marching quickly, Alexander took Phoenicia, Syria, Tyre, then Egypt, which promptly surrendered, placing all its treasuries and grain at his disposal. In fact, Alexander named Egypt, which had previously been known to its inhabitants as Khem. Asia Minor fell quickly, and the Persians were soundly routed at the battles of Granikos and Issus, mysteriously declining to combine all their forces against him until much too late, when a massive battle on the fields of Gaugamela showed them the brilliance of Alexander and the end of their empire. They were finished, and within weeks the Emperor Darius was murdered by his own subjects, who were eager to replace him with this young, godlike king whom no force could seemingly resist.

While building the first of many cities called Alexandria on the coast of Egypt, he began work on the famous library, which became one of the Wonders of the World. But the creator himself did not live to see its completion, or indeed any of his cities, always heading for the next horizon and another conquest.

Passing back through Syria into Persia, he marched up the valley of the Tigris into Mesopotamia and advanced to the Caspian Sea. He had conquered all of Central Asia by 382 B.C., but because he showed no signs of slowing down, his army was becoming increasingly restless. The idealistic warriors who had followed their golden-haired leader had now marched and fought for 6 long years and still saw no sign of returning to their homes and families. Amazingly, they blamed only their officers. Alexander, the driving force behind all their adventures and hardships, was seemingly blameless in their eyes.

Alexander became increasingly authoritarian and began to see himself more as a god, dispensing global solutions. The empire was formed into Greek-like provinces, and its people were commanded to speak Greek and follow Greek customs. Whole Greek populations were relocated to Asia at his command.

Historian Diodorus reliably recorded some of Alexander's plans: "the building of seven great temples to himself, three in Greece, one at Troy, and three in Macedonia, huge population transfers between Europe and Asia, a pyramid dedicated to his father, bigger than anything seen in Egypt, and a fleet of 1,000 triremes to be built for a campaign against Carthage in North Africa," to be followed by the conquest of Africa itself.

Like most of the Greeks of the day, Alexander was occasionally bisexual and delighted in outrageous drinking parties and orgies.

One of his generals, Medius of Larissa, was particularly fond of extremely wild events and introduced Alexander to banquets in which they drank continuously for days on end. Participants stopped only when they became comatose.

In 326 B.C. Alexander launched his conquest of India, which was confined mainly to modern-day Pakistan. But in one particularly vicious battle at Hydaspes against King Porus and his elephants he was nearly killed, although he was finally victorious. In 326 B.C. he founded the city of Bucephala in India, named after his favorite warhorse, Bucephalus, who had died in the battle.

His troops became increasingly depressed by the heavy and continual Indian rains, and not sharing Alexander's passion for infinite novelty and conquest, they finally mutinied on the River Beas. To appease them, he reluctantly turned back down the Indus River to the Arabian Sea. The march back to Persia saw his exhausted army finally begin to crumble. At Opis just outside Babylon, another argument erupted, and although several of his officers were killed, Alexander, whom they still perceived as a god, was never threatened. Regaining control of his troops with huge theatrical gestures of reconciliation and yet another wild banquet, he decided to spend some time reorganizing his empire while his weary troops relaxed and regained their strength and appetite to follow him east for even more conquests.

Unknowingly, Alexander had contracted a form of malaria on the Indian campaign, and although he was only 32, his body had been severely ravaged by more than 15 years of warfare, many serious wounds, and the debauched lifestyle he was committed to.

Although racked by sweats and chills, he allowed his old friend Medius to organize yet another party for him at Babylon in 323 B.C., an event he did not survive. Three days of feasting and drinking took its toll on his weakened frame, and he died in the middle of the night as his loyal troops walked past him in tears, saluting him. His army loved him to the end.

He had led a small force on an unprecedented conquest of the known world, walking thousands of miles into the unknown, and with brilliance, audacity, and the power of his will alone had created one of the biggest empires the world had ever seen. Within months of his death, however, it was already reverting to its original states because he had left no heirs, and his generals squabbled for power, cutting out pieces of the empire for themselves.

Alexander's embalmed corpse was somehow hijacked by his veteran troops while en route to Macedonia. It was displayed in a glass case for almost 550 years in his first city of Alexandria before disappearing from history forever.

MENUS

From an early age, Alexander was brought up to be a soldier and never forgot the staples served at his father's royal court: seafood, lamb, kid, fowl, and fruits. As he grew up, his partying became legendary, with drinking and eating feasts that sometimes went on for days, although throughout his life he maintained a youthful figure. Delicacies from all over the world were available to him, but he still preferred the ancient Greek and Macedonian recipes of his childhood.

Menu

Fired Seafood with Mango and Pepper Relish

Honey-Glazed Lamb

Braised Goat with Leeks and Mushrooms

Swordfish with Sweet and Sour Sauce
and Crushed Mulberries

Sardinian Lobster

Figs with Honey and Wine

Fired Seafood with Mango and Pepper Relish

4 oz extra virgin olive oil
3 tbsp chopped garlic
24 mussels, cooked covered on the grill for about 8 to 10 minutes
4 large shelled scallops
1 large cooked crab with the shell and claws cracked
4 medium-sized squid, cleaned and cut into bite-size pieces
thin strips of lemon and lime for garnish
fresh rosemary or basil to garnish

- Cook the squid and scallops on a barbecue grill for about 4 to 5 minutes each side, covered, so the smoke can penetrate the fish.
- Add the mussels and crab, then combine all the seafood on a large platter. Sprinkle with olive oil and chopped garlic.
- Serve with a mango and pepper relish, and garnish with lemon and lime strips.

Mango and Pepper Relish

3 oz butter
3 finely chopped garlic cloves
1 medium chopped onion
1 tbsp thinly sliced ginger
½ tbsp green chili
½ red pepper, roasted, peeled, and finely chopped
1 tsp olive oil
1 large mango or pawpaw, peeled, stoned, and diced
juice of one lime
2 tbsp shredded fresh mint

- Mix the onion, green chili, and garlic, then add the red pepper, olive oil, diced mango, and lime juice.
- Melt the butter and stir in ginger and garlic.
- Combine all the ingredients, chill, and serve.

Honey-Glazed Lamb

1 large leg of lamb
2 tbsp clear honey
juice of one lemon
2 tbsp chopped fresh coriander
1 tbsp sesame seeds
sea salt and fresh black pepper to taste

- Rub the lamb thoroughly with all other ingredients, then cover with foil and leave for 2 to 3 hours.
- Roast at 400°F for about 2 hours, basting with honey every 30 minutes.
- Let rest for about 20 minutes before slicing and serving.

Braised Goat with Leeks and Mushrooms

Kid or goat is a low-fat item. Goat should be about 1 year old. Look for bright pink meat.

3 lb loin of goat, boned
1 tsp salt
black pepper
2 leeks, sliced
4 oz sliced mushrooms
8 oz dry white wine
lemon rind
1 tbsp plain flour
2 tbsp sour cream

- Season the inside of the meat with half the salt and pepper. Shape into a roll and secure with string.
- Brown in a heavy metal saucepan, then add the leeks and mushrooms and fry for a few minutes.
- Add the rest of the salt and pepper, wine, and lemon rind. Cover with a lid, reduce the heat, and simmer for 1½ to 2 hours until the meat is tender. Remove the lemon and thicken the sauce with a simple flour and water paste. Add sour cream just before serving.

Swordfish with Sweet and Sour Sauce
and Crushed Mulberries

6 large swordfish steaks
2 cups fresh crushed mulberries
2 oz extra virgin olive oil
fresh rosemary
2 cups brown sugar
4 tsp cornstarch, mixed with a little cold water
1 cup white wine vinegar
½ cup freshly squeezed lemon juice
½ cup orange juice
2 tbsp finely chopped capsicum pepper
limes and watercress to garnish

- Lightly oil the swordfish steaks, sprinkle with a little fresh rosemary, and place on a medium grill; cook for about 3 minutes each side.
- In a small pan combine the sugar, vinegar, juices, and pepper, simmer for about 4 minutes, then stir in the corn flour and allow to cook for a couple of minutes.
- Plate up swordfish on a bed of sauce, and spoon 2 cups fresh chilled mulberries on top of the fish. Garnish with limes and watercress.

Sardinian Lobster

2 lobsters, prepared and split
4–6 tbsp dry breadcrumbs
1 garlic clove, finely chopped
6 oz olive oil
juice of 2 lemons
½–1 tbsp herbes de Provence
salt and pepper

- Combine all the ingredients except for the lobsters and bread-crumbs in a bowl to make a marinade.
- Loosen the meat in the lobsters and put half the marinade over each one, then pat down with the breadcrumbs.
- Using medium heat in an oven, or on a grill, cook until lightly browned.
- Serve the remaining sauce on the side.
- Leaving the claws intact, serve on a bed of lettuce with limes.

Figs with Honey and Wine (4)

2 cups dry white wine
⅓ cup clear honey
¼ cup castor sugar
1 small orange
3 whole cloves
1 lb fresh figs, plump and firm
1 cinnamon stick
mint sprigs or bay leaves to garnish
½ pint double cream
1 vanilla pod

- Put the wine, honey, and sugar into a heavy pan and heat gently.
- Stud the orange with the cloves and add to the syrup along with the figs and cinnamon. Cover and simmer gently for 5 to 10 minutes. Remove from heat and cool.
- Heat ¼ pint double cream with a vanilla pod to almost boiling, then leave to cool for 30 minutes.
- Take out the vanilla pod and stir in the remaining cream and ½ tsp castor sugar.

DIANA, PRINCESS OF WALES
Paris, France
August 30, 1997

I will never become Queen. Instead I wish to
become a queen in people's hearts.

—Diana, "Queen of Hearts," November 20, 1993

Despite being born into a royal environment, with her family living on the queen's Sandringham Estate and the queen herself the chief guest at her parents' wedding, Diana Spencer was totally unprepared for the staid and disciplined life of a Windsor royal.

Marrying the heir to the throne, Prince Charles, in a fairytale wedding at St. Paul's Cathedral in front of a worldwide television audience in July 1981 seemed to be a dream come true for her. But although she had two children with the prince, the gap in their ages and many personal differences gradually forced them further and further apart.

With the prince finally confirming his adultery with his long-time consort Camilla Parker-Bowles in a television interview, it was only a matter of time until they separated. In retaliation, Diana gave an interview of her own in 1993, opening the world's eyes to her own unhappiness in the marriage, severe postpartum depression, bulimia, and tense relationship with the rest of the royal family.

Pressured by the queen to accept a divorce from Charles, she eventually agreed, and it was granted on August 28, 1996, a day she later described as "the saddest day of my life."

Away from the restrictive life of the palace and finally single, she threw herself into various charity works, visiting Mother Teresa in 1997 and auctioning off some seventy-nine of her ball gowns for charity, raising more than £3.5 million for the needy.

After years of a loveless marriage, she began to date other men, arriving at one film premiere after another with a string of eligible bachelors. Army Officer James Hewitt was one, and to her horror he wrote a book about their "intimate times." England rugby captain Will Carling was another partner who helped feed the growing tabloid frenzy that followed her everywhere.

Indeed, for someone who had been so shy and reserved on her entrance to public life, she began to relish the glare of the spotlight. Becoming close friends with Gianni Versace, Elton John, and many other celebrities, she seemed to find a way into the newspaper headlines almost every day.

Her long-time butler, Paul Burrell, revealed that she had had an affair with London heart doctor Hasnat Khan for more than 2 years, and he was often smuggled in and out of her palace home in the trunk of a car to visit her.

For all her outward charm, the princess also had several dark aspects to her character. The last years of her life saw her feuding with her family, particularly her brother and mother, whom she didn't speak to for months on end. She had a particularly frosty relationship with the queen's husband, Prince Philip, who had never liked her, and the queen herself, who had taken her son's side against her at every turn.

Although she became very attached to Hasnat Khan, she soon realized that he was not going to be the long-term answer for her, and so she started dating Dodi Fayed, a multimillionaire son of Mohamed Al-Fayed, the owner of Harrods store in London and the Ritz Hotel in Paris.

Although in the last 3 months of her life records show they saw each other only about fourteen times, Diana was continuously dropping hints to the media about their possible long-term future together, which encouraged the paparazzi to follow her even more, eager for the latest gossip.

The morning of Saturday, August 30, 1997, found Diana and Dodi on holiday in Sardinia. Encounters with two photographers caused them to leave their vacation home early, to spend an evening in Paris together.

The arrival of the Fayed customized Gulfstream jet, in the distinctive green and gold colors of the Harrods department store, sent a buzz through the press in Paris, who suspected the couple were on the verge of making a big announcement. Looking for some peace and quiet, the couple, driven by her bodyguard Trevor Rees-Jones, left the airport for a tour of Villa Windsor, a home owned by the Fayeds but once occupied by the Duke and Duchess of Windsor.

Once again they were hounded by the paparazzi on motorcycles, who were determined to get as many pictures as they could of the happy couple, sensing an imminent major announcement.

Having always courted the press, Diana now found she could not escape them, even when she wanted to. So the frustrated couple returned to the Ritz to prepare for their evening together and a romantic dinner at the Bistro Chez Benoit in the Rue Saint-Martin.

Perhaps an indication of Dodi's expectations of the evening was that during the day he had taken possession of a £130,000 diamond solitaire ring he had specially ordered for her some 10 days previously.

Leaving the Ritz for their dinner, they were once again followed by the press, with a dozen motorcycles dogging their every move. They finally decided a quiet night was out of the question and decided to take refuge back at the hotel.

Finally seated for dinner at the famous seafood restaurant L'Esparon, they looked forward to the peaceful end of a long day. But once again nosy onlookers made them unable to really enjoy themselves, so they adjourned to the Imperial Suite to finish their meal. Curiously deciding to finish the evening at Dodi's apartment across Paris, they designed a scheme to give the waiting paparazzi the slip.

Sending decoy cars from the front of the Ritz, they slipped out of the back door at 12:30 A.M. and into a dark Mercedes driven by the assistant of security at the Ritz, Henri Paul, once again accompanied by Diana's bodyguard, Rees-Jones. Their trick didn't work for long. The Mercedes was quickly spotted and enveloped by even more photographers on motorcycles, constantly snapping away.

The Mercedes sped away down the Rue Cambon, heading for the underpass at Place de L'Alma. For some reason Paul kept accelerating to escape the bikes, and just inside the underpass, he lost control. The car hit the side of the tunnel and then the thirteenth central pillar, the impact crushing the front of the car and spinning it around. The driver and Dodi Fayed were killed instantly, and Rees-Jones, the only one wearing a seat belt, sustained terrible injuries to his face and chest.

Diana lay crumpled with serious head and chest injuries, while around the accident the photographers still swarmed, taking flash photographs of the grisly scene.

The first two police officers at the crash stated that some fifteen paparazzi were aggressively preventing them from tending the injured, precious minutes in which Diana could have been treated. It eventually took fire crews more than 1 hour to cut Diana from the wreckage, and although doctors worked on her for more than 2 hours at the Pitié-Salpêtrière Hospital, she was pronounced dead at 4 A.M. that morning.

The whole world was stunned, and England in particular went into a state of shock. Her funeral was the biggest gathering ever in England, and the whole nation mourned her for days. In death, Diana, Princess of Wales, finally became the nation's Queen of Hearts.

MENUS

Princess Diana and Dodi Fayed had their last dinner at the Imperial Suite, Ritz Hotel, Paris.

For Diana

Asparagus and Mushroom Omelet Appetizer

Dover Sole with Vegetables Tempura

For Dodi

Grilled Turbot

Tattinger Champagne

Diana's Favorite Food

Watercress Soup

Asparagus and Mushroom Omelet

4 lightly poached fresh asparagus tips
3 fresh farm eggs
4 oz white sliced button mushrooms
2 oz fresh butter
fresh ground black pepper and sea salt to taste

- Lightly sauté the mushroom slices in 1 oz butter. Keep the asparagus tips warm over a steamer. Melt the remaining butter gently in a 6- to 8-inch omelet pan.
- Beat the eggs; add salt and pepper to taste. When the butter has melted and is getting hot, pour the eggs into the pan. Allow the omelet to get firm by moving the soft portions of the egg from the sides gently to the center using a wooden spatula.

- When it looks sufficiently firm, flip it; this traps oxygen on the omelet's underside and makes the dish extra fluffy. If you think flipping is too risky, place the pan under a hot grill for about a minute. Lay the asparagus and mushroom slices in the center and fold out onto a warm plate in a semicircle shape. Serve with fresh lemon and a sprig of parsley.

Vegetable Tempura (2)

2 medium cucumbers
½ medium eggplant
1 large carrot
½ small yellow onion

For the batter
1 egg
½ cup ice water
½ cup flour
salt and pepper
oil for deep frying

- Using a potato peeler, pare strips of peel from the cucumbers and eggplant to give a striped effect. Cut the vegetables into strips about ⅛ inch wide and 3 to 4 inches long. Place them in a colander and sprinkle with salt, allow to rest for 25 minutes, then rinse under cold water. Drain well.
- Thinly slice the onion from top to base, discarding the center. Separate the strips.
- Mix all the vegetables together and season with salt and pepper.
- Make the batter immediately before frying. Mix the egg and ice water in a bowl, then sift in the flour. Mix briefly with a fork; the batter should be a little lumpy.
- Dip the vegetables in batter, place them one at a time in hot oil, and fry at 350°F for about 3 minutes until golden.
- Serve with salt, slices of lemon, and soy sauce.

Grilled Turbot

4 (8-oz) center slices of turbot
3 oz extra virgin olive oil
1 tsp chopped rosemary
1 tsp chopped thyme
1 finely chopped bay leaf
2 tsp crushed fennel seeds
1 tsp crushed black peppercorns
sea salt

- Preheat the grill to high.
- Mix the oil, herbs, fennel, crushed peppercorns, and 1 tsp sea salt in a bowl, add the turbot and turn so they are well coated.
- Place on an oiled baking tray skin side down and grill for about 7 to 8 minutes.
- Serve with half a lemon and watercress.

Dover Sole (4)

8 double fillets of Dover sole
4 oz butter
½ cup flour
extra virgin olive oil
salt and pepper to taste

- Coat the fish with flour and lightly pat.
- Place ½ the butter and 2 spoons of the oil in a large frying pan on medium heat.
- Shake flour from the fish and fry gently for 3 minutes each side until lightly golden.

Diana's Homemade Watercress Soup

12 oz fresh watercress with large stems removed
2 oz butter
2 oz flour
2 pints chicken stock
1 pint single cream

- Heat butter gently and slowly stir in flour.
- When it is a smooth paste, remove from heat, slowly add stock and watercress, cover, and simmer for 20 minutes.
- Purée in a blender, return to heat, add cream, and serve.

JOHN F. KENNEDY
Dallas, Texas
November 22, 1963

*Ask not what your country can do for you; ask
what you can do for your country.*

—Presidential inaugural address, January 20, 1961

John Fitzgerald Kennedy, the twenty-fifth president of the United States, was born into the wealthy Kennedy family in 1917. Using the family name and money helped him serve three terms in the House of Representatives, running as a Democrat from Massachusetts. On becoming the first Roman Catholic president, he adopted an ambitious and liberal program called the New Frontier and embraced civil rights, admiring the stance of dynamic black leaders such as Martin Luther King. Much of his progressive legislation was eventually blocked by a U.S. Congress that was resistant to any leveling of the playing fields for the country's minorities.

Kennedy summed up his feelings of frustration in a witty way: "The United States Government is sitting down at Geneva in talks with the Soviet Union. I cannot understand why the city council of Albany, Georgia, cannot do the same for its own American citizens."

Within a week of taking office, Kennedy was being guided toward the infamous Bay of Pigs fiasco, a CIA project to remove Castro from power in Cuba. He was assured by his joint chiefs of staff that the Cuban exiles being trained for the invasion were well prepared, even though the force included sixty-year-old Catholic priests, musicians, factory workers, and lawyers. He gave the green light, and the force left the Nicaraguan port of Puerto Cabezas on April 10.

Within 6 days it was all over. Castro had some 1,200 prisoners, and the Kennedy administration was humiliated. Astonishingly, in early May a Gallup poll revealed Kennedy to be more popular than ever, with a whopping 82 percent of the population supporting him. Kennedy quipped to his aides, "It's just like Eisenhower; the worse I do, the more popular I get."

The next year his firm stance against the Soviet Union placing missiles in Cuba brought him even more plaudits, and although the Vietnam war was starting to unravel around him, Kennedy's enthusiastic launch of the space program and creation of the Peace Corps kept Americans' minds focused on what looked like exciting new frontiers for their country and their dynamic, handsome young president.

However, behind the smiling good looks and relaxed demeanor, newly declassified documents reveal a president who went through daily agonies due to severe medical ailments. At one point he was taking eight types of medication a day and eight injections at a time for a naval injury that had shattered three vertebrae in his back. Methadone, codeine, methylphenidate, chlordiazepoxide, gamma globulin, and testosterone were administered daily to control colitis, urinary tract infection, and Addison's disease, a life-threatening condition of the kidneys. The handsome, athletic president the country so looked up to sometimes could not even put on his socks in the morning without assistance. The files show he took painkillers, antianxiety drugs, stimulants, and sleeping pills as well as hormones. And in times of stress he took extra doses.

However, there was one part of his anatomy that seemed to work just fine. For all the medical problems he endured, one aspect that doesn't seem to have been impaired was his sex life. In later years, despite the efforts of his powerful family to keep his reputation pristine, affair after affair finally became public knowledge—most famously of all, his relationship with movie star Marilyn Monroe.

The press of the day loyally refused to pursue any rumors about their hero the president, who was leading America to a brighter tomorrow. The pictures of him and his wife, Jacqueline, always looked the epitome of wedded bliss, and women flocked to have their hair or makeup done "the Jackie way." She would eventually move on from being married to the most powerful man on earth, to being married to the richest—Greek shipping owner Aristotle Onassis.

Kennedy made a tough Texan, Lyndon Johnson, his vice president, and in a move to reduce infighting in the Democratic Party, he elected to take a tour of Texas in late November 1963. Waking up in Fort Worth, Texas, on Friday, November 22, the president stretched and went downstairs for breakfast with local Democratic dignitaries before moving on to Caswell Air Force Base, where he boarded Air Force One, while the Johnson party flew behind in Air Force Two.

When they landed in Dallas on a bright sunny day at 11:39 A.M., a decision was made to leave the bulletproof glass bubble top off the presidential limousine because the temperature was a pleasant 76°F, and the president would have more access to the people eager to see him.

The twenty-four-car motorcade swept through Dallas, with more than 250,000 Texans straining to get a look at their dynamic president. As the convoy moved into Dealey Plaza, 5 minutes from the hotel and lunch, the president was waving his arms at a group of schoolkids when suddenly a shot rang out, followed by another. The president fell forward, and Governor John Connally, who was traveling with him, was also hit. Accelerating away from the ambush the limousine raced to the nearest medical facility. Although they reached the hospital within 6 minutes, President Kennedy was declared dead at 12:55 P.M., to a shocked nation.

To this day the controversy over who killed JFK goes on. A drifter named Lee Harvey Oswald was arrested immediately, but he was himself shot by nightclub owner Jack Ruby only 2 days later. The Warren Commission in 1963 concluded that there could only have been one gunman, but in 1979 another special commission concluded that "there was more than one assassin and a wider conspiracy." Some speculate it was revenge by Castro or the Mafia, or that the CIA was behind the assassination of their own president.

Recent investigations have found that as many as forty-two people connected to the event were murdered or disappeared in the months after Kennedy's death. His relationship with Marilyn Monroe and other women finally came to light, tarnishing the image of the "Camelot" he had sought so hard to project. Thousands of pages of records concerning his murder lie frozen by Congress to this day, implying that the true perpetrators of his death still lie hidden somewhere in top-secret files.

MENUS
John F. Kennedy's last meal in Dallas was a simple breakfast.

Menu
Soft-Boiled Eggs

Bacon, Toast, Marmalade

Orange Juice, Coffee

Favorite Dinner
Hyannis Clam Chowder

Roast Quail Veronique with Mimosa Salad

Stone Crab à la Kennedy

Maltaise Sauce

Hyannis Clam Chowder

4 cups chopped chowder clams; save natural juices
2 cups water
¼ lb salt pork cut into very small pieces
2 diced medium onions
3 cups diced raw potatoes
2 whole cloves
3 tbsp butter
5 cups milk
paprika, salt, and freshly ground black pepper

- Fry the salt pork in a heavy skillet until crisp; remove and set aside.
- Cook the onions in the salt pork fat until golden brown.
- Add the potatoes and the cloves.
- Add the natural juice from the clams and the water.
- Cover and simmer until the potatoes are almost cooked.
- Add the salt pork, clams, and 2 tbsp butter. Simmer for no more than 5 minutes.
- In a separate saucepan, heat the milk to below boiling and pour the chowder into a hot tureen, then add the heated milk, the rest of the butter, and the paprika. Season to taste and serve in heated bowls.

Roasted Quail Veronique

6 dressed quail
½ cup veal bouillon
1½ cup seedless grapes
12 slices bread
1½ cups wild cooked rice
2 tsp melted butter
⅔ cup dry white wine
½ lb boiled Georgia ham

- Preheat oven to 450°F.
- Wash and wipe the quail dry and rub their insides with salt and pepper.
- Stuff each bird with the wild rice mixed with a little of the melted butter and tie with string.
- Place the quail in a shallow roasting pan, brush with butter, and roast for 5 minutes at 450°F. Lower the heat to 325°F and roast for another 20 minutes, basting often with butter.
- When done, remove the birds and keep warm.
- Deglaze the pan with the wine and bouillon and bring to a boil, then add the grapes and let them poach for 5 minutes. Cut the bread and fry in a little butter. Arrange the toast on a serving platter and sprinkle on the ham, julienned.
- Place the quail on top and spoon half the sauce over them. Serve the rest in a sauceboat.

Stone Crabs à la Kennedy

The large claws of the crabs caught on the eastern seaboard of the United States and Florida are delicious when in season.

- Boil them lightly with a dash of seafood spices and a pint of ale.
- Serve cold with maltaise sauce.

Another method:
- Crack the legs, place in shallow baking pan, brush with butter, lemon juice, salt, and pepper, and bake at 350°F for about 8 minutes.

Maltaise Sauce

4 large egg yolks
4 tsp water
2 tsp fresh lemon juice
⅛ tsp hot pepper sauce
8 oz butter, unsalted, melted, and separated
salt and freshly ground pepper to season
1 tbsp orange juice
1 tsp orange zest
1 tsp fresh tarragon leaves, minced

- Melt the butter over a low heat in a saucepan. Let cool slightly.
- Skim the foam from the top of the melted butter. Using a small ladle, carefully remove the clear butter from the saucepan, leaving the remaining milky liquid to discard. Reserve the clarified butter.
- Prepare a double boiler by placing a stainless steel bowl over a pot of lightly simmering water. Do not let the bottom of the bowl touch the water. Add egg yolks, water, and lemon juice, whisking vigorously until the mixture thickens and turns pale yellow. Remove the bowl from the pot.
- Add the clarified butter slowly, while whisking vigorously, until all the butter is incorporated and the sauce has thickened. Whisk in the hot pepper sauce. Season with salt and freshly ground black pepper. Stir in the orange juice, orange zest, and fresh tarragon. Remove from heat, keeping warm until served.

Mimosa Salad (6)

Jacqueline had her own recipe for this dish.

¼ cup olive oil
1 tbsp white wine vinegar
½ tsp salt
dash of pepper
⅓ clove minced garlic
2 large heads of Boston bibb lettuce
2 hard-boiled eggs, finely chopped

- Combine oil, vinegar, salt, pepper, and garlic in a jar with a tight lid. Shake vigorously.
- Arrange greens in salad bowl. Add dressing, toss thoroughly, and sprinkle with chopped egg. (You can also add fresh orange segments.)

MONTEZUMA II,
LAST AZTEC EMPEROR
Tenochtitlan
June 30, 1520

For each meal his servants prepared him more than thirty dishes which they put over small earthenware braziers to prevent them getting cold. They cooked more than three hundred plates of the food the ruler was going to eat, and more than a thousand more for his guards. Every day they cooked fish, turkey, pheasants, duck, venison, pigeons, hares and rabbits. When he began his meal they placed a small screen in front of him, so that none should see him eat.

—Bernal Díaz, conquistador, from
True History of the Conquest of New Spain, 1565

In 1502, while becoming the first European to eat turkey after running into a tribe of Maya Indians in the Gulf of Honduras, Christopher Columbus decided to follow the winds and headed south, not knowing that, had he followed the Indians northward to the Yucatán Peninsula, he would have found riches and a civilization far greater than anything he had ever dreamed about: the fabulous Aztec Empire.

Situated in the heart of the valley of Mexico and surrounded by a large lake was the island city of Tenochtitlan, capital city of an empire that held sway from the Pacific Ocean to the Gulf of Mexico and southwards into Guatemala. Mighty pyramids and more than thirty great palaces graced the city, with its well laid-out canals, causeways, and flower gardens. The population of more than 300,000 lived in well-ordered houses with running water latrines, a luxury unheard of in Europe.

The great markets, selling goods from all over the empire, had more than 25,000 traders every day, selling a variety of goods that were unknown in Europe at the time but are staples of our diet today. Squash, tomatoes, limes, peanuts, turkeys, pineapples, chewing gum, rubber, vanilla, chocolate, avocados, potatoes, watermelon, corn, and many others were arguably the greatest treasures the Aztecs ever gave up.

In 1518 the power and wealth of this great civilization were centered around one man, the *tlatoani* or emperor, Montezuma II. After leading his people for many years as a fierce and ruthless warlord, Montezuma had ascended to the throne in 1502. He expanded the empire rapidly, and unknowingly, through his harsh treatment of conquered tribes, he sowed the seeds of his nation's destruction.

In the years after Columbus's meetings with the Maya Indians, Spanish explorers from Cuba had increasingly encroached along the coastline until in early spring 1519, the most ruthless and cunning of them all landed on the Yucatán Peninsula, the conquistador Hernán Cortés.

Cortés brought 500 heavily armored conquistadors, cannons, and horses, which the Indians described as "half man, half dog" because they had never seen cavalry. He sought through any means to discover the gold they all dreamed of. At every turn they heard of a shimmering city over the mountains and the power of the emperor who ruled it. Using natives who had met Spanish people before as his interpreters, Cortés laid a dual strategy, crushing any resistance with sharp Toledo steel but also promising any tribe who joined him complete freedom from their Aztec masters.

From the minute of Cortés's arrival, Montezuma received regular reports about these mysterious white men with beards, and although he could have obliterated them at any time, he had become very superstitious and wary. The Aztec calendar revolved every 52 years, and the legends told of a bearded white god who would return over the waters in the year "one-reed." By coincidence, this was that year. Could these be the promised ones of legend? Unsure, he adopted a policy of observing these strangers from afar and sending minor chiefs to ask what they were looking for.

Cortés, for his part, couldn't really fly his true colors. So he represented himself as an ambassador of a mighty king instead of the booty-loving adventurer he really was. As his allied forces grew rapidly, he finally got up the courage to move inland, and so on the morning of November 8, 1519, Cortés, some 300 conquistadors, and more than 3,000 native troops were greeted at the main causeway into Tenochtitlan by the Emperor Montezuma II himself.

The Spanish were staggered by the gleaming city with a circumference of some 9 miles and even more so by the numbers of fierce warriors around them. They felt real fear. However, Montezuma was intrigued and taken with these never-before-seen strangers with their curious clothes and language. And the legend of bearded white men returning to claim power was always at the back of his mind.

For many years Montezuma had been held in such awe by his people that they did not even raise their eyes to look at him, and simply touching him meant death. Now these strangers looked him boldly in the eye and touched him about his hands and face, gestures that infuriated Montezuma's nobles. But he restrained them and ordered Cortés and his forces to be quartered in the palace of Axayactl, directly across from his own residence, a huge building that covered more than 6 acres.

Over the next few days Cortés was lavishly entertained by the emperor, who saw no threat from such a small force and appeared to have been fascinated by them. But the Spaniards were getting increasingly nervous, seeing the human sacrifices night after night on the pyramids around them and conscious of the huge forces around them that needed only a nod to seal their fate.

Now Cortés took his boldest step: On November 14 he sought an audience with Montezuma for himself, several officers, and thirty men. The unsuspecting emperor greeted his guest warmly, only to be taken aback when Cortés threatened him with instant death if he didn't come with him immediately. The startled Montezuma, not realizing what was happening to him, told his court that he had been visited by the gods and told to stay with the Castilians for a little while, and he moved himself and a part of his court into Cortés's hands.

Cortés had pulled off a brilliant coup: He would allow Montezuma to seemingly control the empire, but he himself would control Montezuma.

For many weeks the strategy seemed to work, Montezuma continued with his normal lifestyle of taking daily baths, changing his clothing ritually four times a day, and appointing judges and other nobles as the occasion demanded. Every evening he ascended to the roof of the palace to shed his blood at midnight in honor of the North Star and important constellations of the Aztec race.

But behind the scenes, Montezuma, the wall behind which his people took shelter, was losing the affection of those same people as they began to see the hand of the uncouth strangers behind every utterance from Montezuma's mouth.

Problems began to mount, and although Montezuma still ate his favorite seafood brought by runner every day from the Gulf of Mexico, the people were ready to revolt. The chance came when Cortés left the city to confront a rival Spaniard and left his deputy, Pedro de Alvarado, in command, a decision he came to regret because Alvarado believed force was the only way to treat the natives. As Cortés left the city Alvarado saw his chance to finally cow the heathen population.

The Aztecs were having a large festival in the Great Square where many lords, singers, and dancers, all unarmed, were attacked and slaughtered without warning by Alvarado's troops, who had become very fearful of such numbers around them. The artillery and slashing swords against unprotected bodies wreaked dreadful havoc. Powerless to prevent the massacre of his people, Montezuma had finally lost their love and respect forever.

Returning to the capital after defeating his rival, Narváez, and incorporating his troops with his own forces, Cortés immediately sensed new dangers around him.

The Aztecs were becoming increasingly confrontational, and

although Montezuma was still treated with some reverence, that too was waning. By June 30, 1520, the Spanish were virtually besieged in their palace. In desperation Cortés sent Montezuma to the palace roof that evening to plead with the people massed below.

They listened quietly for a while, then a rock hit Montezuma, and then another; the Spanish rushed him below, where he was garroted along with thirty of his nobles, and his broken body was thrown to the crowd. The reign of Montezuma II was over. That night Cortés elected to make a dash for the mainland. Loading themselves with as much gold as they could carry, the Spanish army and its allies tried to quietly exit the city.

Within minutes thousands of waiting Aztec warriors, wearing cotton armor and headdresses of eagles and jaguars, swarmed over them. Many Spaniards jumped into the lake, only to be drowned by the weight of their plunder, and many others were hacked apart by the obsidian-edged weapons of the Aztecs. A weeping Cortés staggered from the city at fearful cost.

In what is known as the Noche Triste ("Sorrowful Night"), all Cortés's native allies were slain, along with more than 1,000 Spanish troops, more than two thirds of his command. It was the largest defeat ever suffered by European armies in the Americas. Some 270 Spaniards in another part of the city were never even told of the escape attempt and joined other captured troops nightly on the sacrificial stones of the great pyramids.

The Aztecs, who were not used to fighting wars of extermination, let Cortés and his survivors retreat to the coast, where he eventually rebuilt his forces and moved once again on their capital. By now smallpox, brought in by Cortés's troops from Cuba, had hit the Aztec population and killed many thousands of the warriors and citizens, who had no immunity to it. But even without an emperor they fought on, forcing Cortés to reduce the city block by block to defeat them. Today Mexico City is built on the remains of that fabulous empire.

MENUS

Even in the days before his death on June 30, 1520, Montezuma was still being treated as a deity. Although his Spanish captors were being subjected to ever-increasing hostility by the Aztecs, the daily ritual of court life for Montezuma went on. He drank chocolate from golden goblets and enjoyed his favorite seafoods, brought every day by runners from the Gulf of Mexico.

Seviche of Red Snapper (6)

2 lb red snapper, skinned, filleted, cut in thin lozenge shapes
12 fresh limes, juiced
2 tomatoes, blanched, skinned, and diced
2 stalks finely chopped celery
1 green pepper, seeded, finely chopped
¼ cup fresh cilantro, chopped
¼ cup fresh chopped parsley
¼ cup extra virgin olive oil
salt and pepper to taste

- Rinse the snapper well, then place it in an earthenware or glass bowl, pour the lime juice over the fish, and stir. Cover with foil and refrigerate for 12 hours.
- Drain off about half the juice from the bowl, stir in all the other ingredients gently. Serve with a background of limes, avocados, tomatoes, and tortilla chips. Eat with lime and chili salsa.

Lime and Chili Salsa (6)

18 limes, peeled and segmented
8 large garlic cloves, chopped
6 large Ancho chilis
1 large white onion
1 bunch chopped cilantro
18 tomatillos, chopped

- Place the chilis in a warm oven for a few minutes until they expand, then chop finely. Leaving the seeds in makes it hotter, so be careful.
- Combine all the other ingredients in a bowl with 1 tbsp vinegar, adding the chilis a little at a time to get the correct taste. Refrigerate for at least 6 hours before serving.

Roasted Turkey Breast with Sage and Apricots (6)

2 turkey breasts with skin on
2 tsp chopped rosemary
salt and pepper to taste
6 large apricots, sliced thickly
6 figs
large bunch fresh sage; chop half

- Remove skin from the turkey breasts and rub them well with the chopped sage, the rosemary, salt, and pepper.
- Place slices of apricot and figs over the breasts, attaching them with cocktail sticks. Place skin back on, over cocktail sticks, or omit skin if preferred.
- Roast for 2½ hours in 325°F oven, covering with foil after breasts brown.
- Garnish with fresh sage.

Tomato, Avocado, and Jicama Salad (4)

Jicama is a Mexican potato, which can grow to the size of an American football. It is dark brown in color and when peeled has a consistency similar to that of the water chestnut.

    1 large jicama, peeled and thinly sliced
    3 tsp balsamic vinegar
    3 large avocados, peeled and sliced
    3 large tomatoes, sliced
    6 tbsp olive oil
    1 finely chopped white onion
    salt and pepper to taste

- Whisk together the oil, vinegar, and seasoning; add the lime juice and jicama.
- Lay alternating slices of avocados and tomatoes on a plate and spoon the jicama dressing on top. Finish with a sprinkling of chopped onions.

Guacamole (4)

2 large avocados, roughly chopped
1 chopped, seeded habanera chili
2 finely chopped spring onions
1 tbsp chopped fresh coriander
2 tbsp extra virgin olive oil juice
1 fresh lime
salt and pepper to taste

- Combine all the ingredients gently in a glass bowl; refrigerate for 2 hours.
- Serve with jicama salad and roast turkey.

Spicy Hot Chocolate

Montezuma reportedly drank up to 50 goblets of this a day. He considered it a great aphrodisiac.

12 oz finely ground chocolate
12 tsp drinking chocolate
2 pints water
8 tsp honey
4 tsp vanilla flavor
1 tsp red chili, finely chopped

- Blend all ingredients for 1 minute.
- Add 6 shots of tequila for nonvirgin version.
- The only real alcoholic drink the Aztecs had was called *pulque*, which was made from the pulp of the maguey cactus. For these dishes I recommend Dos Equis or Tecate, excellent Mexican beers, and of course tequila.

RASPUTIN
St. Petersburg, Russia
December 20, 1916

*I write and leave behind me this letter at St. Petersburg. I feel that I
shall leave life before 1 January. If I am killed by common assassins,
and especially by my brothers the Russian peasants, you, Tsar of
Russia, have nothing to fear, remain on your throne and govern and
you, Russian Tsar, will have nothing to fear for your children. They will
reign for hundreds of years in Russia. If it be your relations who wrought
my death, then no one will remain alive for more than two years.*

—Letter from Rasputin to Tsar Nicolas II, 1915
(delivered posthumously)

Within months of Rasputin's death his prophecy was fulfilled: The
Russian Revolution of 1917 wiped the Russian imperial family
from the pages of history.

Born in Torboisk, Siberia, in 1872, Grigori Yefimovich Rasputin led the typical life of many peasants of the day, uneducated and
scrabbling for a living on his feudal lord's land with little apparent
future. One day, without any warning, he thrust his shovel into the
grain he was threshing and marched off.

Walking from village to village for more than a year, he claimed he had a vision to seek religious enlightenment. When he returned to his home town he was a changed man. He took to living in a cave, often beating his head against the floor with his newfound zeal. Seemingly from out of nowhere, he claimed he had developed the power of prophecy and healing, also instructing himself in the art of hypnosis.

He began to cross the country on long pilgrimages, using his talents to heal the peasantry and simultaneously using them for his growing sexual appetites. He developed a reputation as a mystic. Expounding the belief that it was necessary to sin in order to obtain forgiveness, he began to build a national name until finally his outrageous behavior brought him to the attention of the Russian rulers, Tsar Nicholas II and Tsarina Alexandra.

On arriving at the imperial court, Rasputin immediately used all his charms and cunning to ingratiate himself with the royal couple. Settling into his role as a devout holy man, he cultivated a meek and radiant demeanor as he sought to develop his influence with his royal benefactors.

Almost immediately, he found the ideal opportunity: Crown Prince Alexei had hemophilia. Even the slightest injury caused the prince to bleed profusely, and no doctor of the court was able to stop it. Each little incident weakened the prince even more, and his despairing parents saw that his end could not be far away. However, Rasputin was somehow able to use his powers of hypnosis to immediately stop the bleeding. A delighted Alexandra took him into her closest circle of advisors and kept him near her at all times. He had saved her son. This was the opening Rasputin needed. With the tsar now concentrating on the upcoming world war, Rasputin was able, through the tsarina, to place all his followers in the highest positions of church and state. Jealous rivals simply "disappeared" or "retired."

His sinister power and advocacy of sexual ecstasy as a means of religious salvation horrified the nobles of St. Petersburg, who saw their own influence slipping away. The tsarina would hear no words against her new favorite. Even when the head of the Secret Police compiled a report detailing Rasputin's excesses, the tsar ignored it, and Alexandra dismissed it as jealousy.

Because Alexei's illness had to be kept from the public, everyone assumed Rasputin was the tsarina's lover, an illusion he did nothing to dispel. He began calling the tsar "Papa" and his wife "Mama," so sure was he of his power over them and his permanent place in the royal court.

As much as the nobility hated him, he was curiously loved by most of the Russian peasantry, who viewed him as their champion and as the last hope they had of influencing the imperial family to change the wretched lives they led. But his constant meddling with the tsar's decisions began to cripple the imperial government, and with war approaching with Germany, many nobles suspected that he might even be a German spy.

Alexandra refused to listen to anyone, looking only at the fact that she believed without him her darling little son would surely die. There were many examples of Rasputin's uncanny ability to perform his "miracles." In 1914, when the royal train was involved in a wreck, the lady Anya Vyrvlova sustained life-threatening injuries. As she lay unconscious in the guardroom with both legs broken, a fractured skull, and numerous other injuries, Rasputin, his eyes bulging out of their sockets with strain, whispered gently in her ear, "Anyushka, wake up, look at me." She did, quickly revived, and was healed in a very short time.

The damage he was doing to the state could not be ignored, however, and two of Nicholas's own cousins devised a solution to the nation's problems. Princes Dmitri Pavlovich and Felix Yusupov decided to put their plan into effect on the cold winter night of December 20.

Rasputin made no attempt to hide his sexual obsessions, often sitting in taverns with his trousers unzipped while he groped anyone within reach before dragging them to his drunken orgies, safe in the knowledge that no one could touch him. So they decided that sex would be the bait for the princes' trap.

Rasputin had long coveted the wife of one of the princes, the Lady Irina Yusupov, and luring him to the Yusupov palace where Irina was promised to him as a "dessert," they sat in the wine cellar with others for a drunken banquet.

Rasputin had a prodigious appetite for food and drink, and that night was no exception. Unaware that his wine and cakes were heavily laced with poison he drank on, constantly asking, "When will I get Irina?" Eventually a frustrated Felix, seeing that the poison had no effect, shot him at close range, and Rasputin collapsed to the floor, lying as if dead. The princes went upstairs to organize the disposal of the body and celebrate a good night's work and the salvation of the royal couple.

Deciding to return to the cellar to look for any documents that Rasputin might have on him, Felix was horrified to find himself seized with incredible strength by a suddenly revived Rasputin. Breaking away, he raced up the stairs, shouting for Dmitri to come and help him, but when they returned to the cellar Rasputin was gone. Frantically they followed a blood trail outside, where they found him crawling to a side gate. Kicking, beating, and shooting him repeatedly, they at last believed him dead, so binding his arms and legs, they rolled him in a carpet and threw him into the freezing Neva River, which ran along the side of the palace.

Incredibly, Rasputin's body was found the next day on the banks of the river with his restraints broken, and the ensuing autopsy showed his lungs were full of water, meaning that after all they did to him that night, he actually died of drowning.

Although the nobility of the country enjoyed their liberation from "the monster," the common people mourned him. The revolution quickly gathered pace, and within months the whole Romanov family was murdered by Stalin and his revolutionists. The prophecies of Rasputin were fulfilled to the letter.

MENUS

Last Meal

Honeyed Cakes

Madeira Wine

Zakuski

Russian Black Bread

The range of Zakuski is infinite, from simple smoked sprats to Beluga caviar, savory stuffed eggs, or tender kidneys in Madeira sauce; they are an integral part of any Russian gathering.

Favorite Foods

Codfish Soup

Pickled Cabbage

Borscht

Sturgeon in Champagne Sauce

Zakuski

Honeyed Cakes

To make 24 2-inch cakes. This recipe dates from 1872.

8 tbsp butter
4 cups flour
3 tbsp superfine sugar
2 tbsp honey
1½ tbsp baking powder
1 egg yolk
1 whole egg + one white of the egg, lightly beaten
1 cup milk
salt

For honey topping:
1 cup heather honey
3 tbsp almonds, blanched and ground

- In a bowl, rub the butter into the flour. In another bowl add the milk.
- In a saucepan over low heat, gently heat the sugar and honey until well mixed. Then stir in the baking powder. Alternatively, add the honey mixture, the eggs, and the milk to the flour, mixing the ingredients very well. Add a pinch of salt and put the resulting dough on a floured board; roll it very lightly to about ½ inch.
- Cut out about 24 rounds. Place the rounds on a buttered baking tray in a preheated oven for about 20 minutes or until they are brown. Remove the cakes to a rack. Put the rack of cakes in a 250°F oven for no longer than 5 minutes to set. The cakes can be served either hot or cold.

Baked Sturgeon

1 sturgeon
1 oz sour cream
salt and pepper
¼ oz shredded cheese
½ oz fat

For garnish:
2 oz fresh or pickled cucumbers
2 oz tomatoes
sliced lemon
½ oz greens

- Preheat the oven to 480 to 540°F.
- Cut the fish into pieces. Grease the frying pan with fat.
- Spread sour cream over the fish and sprinkle with cheese. Add salt and pepper to taste. Bake the fish until it is ready.
- Serve with vegetables and greens.

Codfish Soup

2 small whole cod
1 cup milk
1 cup heavy cream
salt and pepper to taste

- Cut fish into 2-inch pieces; add milk and cream. Simmer gently, without boiling, until the fish is tender. Season and serve with toasted bread.

Pickled Cabbage

1 cabbage, shredded
1 squash, cubed

For marinade:
2 quarts water
3 cups sugar
2 tbsp vinegar
2 tbsp oil
4 tbsp salt

- Blanch vegetables for 5 minutes and cool them in cold water. Drain and put in a sterilized jar and then pour in the marinade.
- Allow to cool and then refrigerate.

Borscht (10)

1 cup navy beans, dry
2½ lb lean beef
½ lb slab bacon
10 cups water
1 bay leaf
8 whole peppercorns
2 cloves garlic
2 tbsp dried parsley
1 carrot
1 celery stalk
1 large red onion
1 tsp salt, optional
8 large beets for soup
2 small beets
2 cups green cabbage, shredded
2 large leeks, sliced
3 medium potatoes, cut into eighths
1 tbsp tomato paste
3 tbsp wine vinegar
4 tbsp sugar
1 lb kielbasa, optional
2 tbsp flour
1 tbsp butter, melted
½ cup sour cream, optional

- Cover the beans with water and allow them to soak overnight, then cook them until tender and drain before setting aside. Place the beef, bacon, and water in a large soup pot and bring to a boil. Skim any fat from the surface. Add the bay leaf, peppercorns, garlic, parsley, carrot, celery, onion, and salt. Cover and simmer over a low heat for about 1 to 1½ hours.
- Scrub the large beets for the soup and cook them in boiling water until tender, about 45 minutes. Drain and discard water and let them cool. Peel and cut each beet into eighths. Scrub the small beets, grate them, and cover with cold water to soak.
- Remove the meat from the soup and set aside. Strain the soup into another pot and add the cooked beets, cabbage, leeks, potatoes, tomato paste, vinegar, sugar, beef, and bacon. Bring to a boil and simmer for 45 minutes.
- Cut kielbasa into chunks and add along with the navy beans to the soup. Simmer 20 minutes.
- Mix flour and butter together to form a paste. Stir into soup to thicken it slightly. Strain the raw beets, saving the liquid and discarding the beets. Add the beet liquid to soup.
- Additional sugar or vinegar may be added for sweeter or sourer flavor. Slice the meats and arrange in individual soup bowls. Pour the hot soup with vegetables over the meat. Garnish each serving with a dollop of sour cream, if desired.

Zakuski (Zesty Eggplant Slices) (6)

1¾ lb long, narrow eggplants, cut into ½-inch slices
1 tbsp coarse kosher salt
4 large cloves garlic, crushed in a garlic press
3 tbsp red wine vinegar
½ cup olive oil, or as needed
¼ cup cilantro, chopped
freshly ground black pepper and salt to taste

- Place the eggplant slices in a colander and toss with the salt. Let stand for 30 minutes. Rinse the eggplant well under cold running water and pat dry with a kitchen towel.
- In a small bowl, combine the garlic and vinegar and let stand while you cook the eggplant.
- Divide the oil between 2 large skillets and heat until it sizzles. Add eggplant slices to both skillets, without overcrowding, and fry until a deep golden on both sides, 12 to 15 minutes. Repeat with any remaining slices.
- Transfer the fried slices to a large bowl, without draining. Let cool.
- Place the cooled eggplant slices in a serving dish in layers, sprinkling each layer with vinegar and garlic mixture, pepper, salt if needed, and cilantro.
- Cover and refrigerate for at least 2 hours before serving.

Russian Pickled Whitefish (4)

4 pieces whitefish fillet, about 6 oz each
1 onion, thinly sliced
1 tbsp mustard
1 tsp whole coriander seed
1 tsp minced garlic
1 cup white wine
¼ cup vinegar
¼ cup water
2 tbsp chopped fresh dill
salt and pepper to taste

- Preheat oven to 375°F.
- Place the whitefish in a baking dish just large enough to hold the fillets, then spread the onions over the top and set aside.
- Combine the mustard, coriander, garlic, wine, vinegar, water, dill, salt, and pepper in a small pan. Place over high heat, quickly bring to a boil, and pour over the whitefish fillets.
- Cover the baking dish and place in the oven for 5 minutes.
- Remove from the oven, let cool to room temperature, and place in the refrigerator.
- Serve chilled.

Oat Bran Russian Black Bread (1)

3 tbsp dried yeast
1 tsp Sucanat
1 cup warm water
¾ cup rye flour
2 cup whole wheat flour
1 tsp salt
1 cup oat bran
1 tbsp carob or cocoa powder
1 tsp caraway seeds
1 tsp fennel seeds
2 tbsp cider vinegar
2 tbsp dark molasses
2 tbsp corn oil
1 tbsp minced onion

- Dissolve yeast and Sucanat in about ½ cup water and set aside until the yeast is foamy.
- Combine rye flour, whole wheat flour, salt, oat bran, carob or cocoa, and caraway and fennel seeds.
- In a separate bowl, combine the vinegar, molasses, oil, and onion.
- Add the wet ingredients to the dry ingredients and blend well.
- Add yeast and mix well. If the dough is too stiff or dry, add more water. If too sticky, add more flour.
- Turn the dough out onto a floured surface, flatten it out, and shape it into a round, shallow loaf. Place the loaf onto a lightly oiled baking sheet, brush dough with oil, and let it rise in a warm spot until the dough holds an imprint when gently touched, about 30 minutes.
- Bake at 375°F for 35 to 40 minutes and let cool on a wire rack. Lightly brush the top with flavored oil.

CLEOPATRA
Alexandria, Egypt
August 6, 30 B.C.

For Rome, who had never condescended to fear any nation or people, did in
her time fear two human beings, one was Hannibal and the other a woman.

—Plutarch

Cleopatra VII was born in Alexandria, Egypt, in 69 B.C. In the next
forty years until her death, she would seduce two rulers of the
mighty Roman Empire and have their children, before finally going
down in the pages of history as the last Pharaoh of Egypt.

Cleopatra's ancestor was Ptolemy I. He had been a general of
the fabled Alexander the Great and became ruler of Egypt on Alexander's death in 323 B.C. The Ptolemy pharaohs were proud of
their Macedonian and Greek heritage, and when Cleopatra finally
ascended the throne at the age of 17, one of the things her subjects
most admired about her was that she was the first pharaoh in nearly
300 years to actually speak Egyptian.

Ancient coins, and what few drawings remain of her, show a
masculine-looking woman with a long hooked nose. Daily baths in
milk did nothing to improve her features, but diligent study made

85

her fluent in nine languages and a very shrewd politician. She had an extremely musical voice and exuded a sexuality that she was always prepared to use to further her ambitions.

In keeping with Egyptian and Ptolemaic tradition, Cleopatra married her brother Ptolemy XIII when he was about 12. For 3 years he was forced to remain in the background, but eventually, goaded by jealous palace eunuchs, he tried to seize the throne from her in 48 B.C., and she was forced to flee to Syria for help.

Fate came to her aid. Julius Caesar had just defeated Pompey the Great for total control of the Roman Empire at the Battle of Pharsalos in Greece. The defeated Pompey had fled to Alexandria, hotly pursued by Caesar, to ask for Ptolemy XIII's protection. Seeking to curry favor with the oncoming Caesar, Ptolemy killed Pompey and proudly presented his head in a wine jug. Although they were opposing generals, Pompey had once been Caesar's good friend, and he was appalled at his brutal treatment. Caesar took control of the city and ordered both Ptolemy and Cleopatra to meet him so he could decide who would eventually rule Egypt.

Knowing Ptolemy would try to have her murdered before she could address Caesar, Cleopatra had herself smuggled in front of him rolled up in an oriental rug. Impressed by her ingenuity and bewitched by her charm, Julius Caesar became her lover that night. Within 6 months a defeated Ptolemy was found drowned in the Nile, and the undisputed reign of Egypt's last pharaoh was under way.

Giving birth to Caesar's son, named Caesarion or "little Caesar," Cleopatra was now at the height of her powers. Although her lover returned to Rome to reorganize the Senate there, he left three of his veteran legions to protect her throne, and a year later he brought her to Rome to celebrate his war triumphs. One of the spoils of the war was Cleopatra's sister Arsinoë, who in the true Ptolemaic tradition was constantly trying to usurp Cleopatra.

An indication of Cleopatra's ruthlessness is that although Caesar eventually spared Arsinoë's life, Cleopatra later made Mark Antony kill her.

Cleopatra and Caesar lived together in Rome for 2 years, even though Caesar was already married to Calpurnia. Caesar was ready to proclaim himself king of the republic and pass a law allowing him to marry Cleopatra, with Caesarion as the heir to the throne of Rome.

Too many self-serving senators stood to lose their power if this happened, and so on March 15, 44 B.C., Julius Gaius Caesar was brutally murdered at a Senate meeting. Knowing that she too was in imminent danger, Cleopatra returned at once to Alexandria and made her son Caesarion her co-regent.

Caesar's sudden death led to civil war in Rome. Eventually three men assumed control: one of Caesar's best friends and his nephew, Mark Antony; Caesar's great-nephew Octavian, who later became the great Emperor Augustus; and Marcus Lepidus.

Looking into Caesar's death, Antony and Cleopatra met in Tarsus in 42 B.C. What was originally a fact-finding mission for the Roman turned into a love affair, as the charms of Cleopatra captivated the rugged Antony. When he finally shook himself free to return to his duties as co-ruler of the Roman Empire, he left Cleopatra with their twins, Cleopatra Selene and Alexander Helios. They were apart for 4 years until, in 37 B.C. on his way to war with Parthia, Antony met up with Cleopatra again and declared his undying love for her. Making the city of Alexandria his home, he then had another son by her, called Ptolemy Philadelphus. Actually, in his time away from Cleopatra, Antony had also married Octavian's half-sister Octavia and had two more daughters with her, both named Antonia.

The wily Octavian now started to turn the people of Rome against Antony in his absence, seeing a chance to rule Rome alone.

Antony, completely under Cleopatra's spell, pronounced his children with her the new kings of Armenia and Syria and his daughter the new queen of Crete and Cyrenaica. Cleopatra herself became the "Queen of Kings."

This was all Octavian needed, a challenge to the authority of Imperial Rome, and the people rose behind him as he sought a quick defeat of Antony and his Egyptian harlot.

In 31 B.C. Octavian's navy defeated the ships of Antony at the Battle of Actium, and a depressed Antony returned to Alexandria to party away his final days in a drunken stupor.

Determined to press his advantage, Octavian followed, and in 30 B.C. he and his army reached Alexandria, causing Antony's remaining troops to just melt away, unwilling to fight against fellow Romans in order to defend an Egyptian queen.

Believing Cleopatra to be already dead, a distraught Antony stabbed himself in the stomach but didn't kill himself; he actually died in front of Cleopatra. With Octavian determined to march her as his prisoner through the streets of Rome in his triumph, and seeing her last lover die in front of her, Cleopatra sought to convince Octavian that she would play along with him, so he would relax his guard over her.

Organizing a sumptuous banquet to feign normalcy, she had a cobra smuggled in with the food in a basket of figs. Then, with the aid of her maids Chamion and Iras, she committed suicide. A furious Octavian, robbed of his prize, found her stretched out in her quarters on a golden tomb. The time of the pharaoh was over.

MENUS

Although she put on an elaborate banquet to fool the Romans into believing she was cooperating with them, Cleopatra herself always ate very healthfully, with the accent on seafood.

Menu

Grilled Eel with Basil

Whole Baked Fish in Salt Crust

Tiger Nut Sweets

Sweet Wine Cakes

Hummus

Grilled Eel with Basil (4)

Considered a sacred fish of the Nile.

4 eels of about 1 lb each
4 tsp balsamic vinegar
8 oz fresh basil leaves, chopped
3 tbsp olive oil

- Rub the eel skins with a pumice stone or rigid cloth. Wash and gut the eels, and then remove the heads and split the bodies open. Marinate for about 1 hour with the olive oil and basil.
- Cut the eels; crossways, with slices about 3 inches long. Place the pieces on the grill, skin side down. No other condiment is necessary, as the fat of the fish will give it an additional taste.
- Cook for 4 to 5 minutes each side, then brush with balsamic vinegar and serve.

Whole Fish in Salt Crust (4)

1 whole snapper, 6 lb, or same size sea bass, cleaned and gutted
4 egg whites
2 cups kosher salt
1 large bunch fresh thyme
4 tbsp extra virgin olive oil
1 lemon cut into wedges

- Heat oven to 450°F.
- Whisk egg whites and set aside. Place 4 tbsp egg white on a large platter suitable for oven-to-table use. Insert the salt and thyme inside the raw fish. Place the fish on top of the mixture and spoon the remaining mixture over the top of the fish. Place the coated fish in the oven and bake for 25 to 30 minutes.
- Remove the salted crust from the fish and fillet. Serve with a splattering of good olive oil and lemon wedges.

Tiger Nut Sweets

- Chop 7 oz fresh dates fine and blend with a little water. Add a little cinnamon and chopped walnuts. Shape into balls, coat in honey and ground almonds, and serve.

Sweet Wine Cakes

15 oz flour
1 tbsp sweet wine
pinch cumin
pinch aniseed
2 oz fat
1 oz finely chopped cheese
1 beaten egg
12 bay leaves

- Add wine to the flour along with the cumin and aniseed.
- Rub in the fat and the cheese and blend with the egg.
- Shape into 12 small cakes and place each on a bay leaf.
- Bake for 25 to 30 minutes at 400°F.

Hummus

8 oz chickpeas
2 tbsp wine vinegar
3 cloves chopped garlic
5 tbsp sesame seed oil
1 tsp sea salt

- Cook and mash the chickpeas.
- Add vinegar, salt, chopped garlic, and sesame seed oil to make a unique paste for bread or savories.
- Chill and serve.

ADMIRAL HORATIO NELSON
HMS *Victory*, Trafalgar, Spain
October 21, 1805

England expects every man today to do his duty.

—Rear Admiral Horatio Nelson,
message to fleet, October 21, 1805

Born as a sickly child in the sleepy English town of Burnham Thorpe in Norfolk in 1758, Horatio Nelson was one of only three children who survived of the eleven his mother bore. Exhausted, she died at the age of 42, leaving a distraught Nelson unsure of his future life.

By the age of 11 he had found the answer, the sea, enrolling first on a relative's ship and then as a junior office at the age of 14 in the British Navy, an institution he came to consider his only real family.

By the age of 16 he had already been to the Arctic, India, and the West Indies, and in his 2 years' service he had witnessed some 200 floggings, as the Royal Navy enforced a harsh, rigorous discipline on crews that had been mainly press-ganged into service or dredged from local jails.

These earlier experiences, coupled with the death of his mother, made him determined to improve the lot of his men when he had his own command, something he believed he was destined to do.

By the age of 21 he had become one of the youngest ever captains in the Royal Navy's history, combining a clear tactical eye and love of the sea with a kindness to his men that commanded unwavering respect and loyalty. Even in the hours of England's most famous victory at Trafalgar, the diaries of his fellow captains reflected only sadness at his death, not glory in their victory.

Already frail to begin with, his constitution was further undermined by the loss of sight in his right eye in a battle off Corsica, then the loss of his right arm in further action at Santa Cruz in the Canary Islands.

Neither injury was referred to in anything but jest. Indeed, when one landlady in Great Yarmouth asked him whether she could name her pub after him, wanting to call it The Nelson Arms, he laughed it off, saying "Shouldn't it be the Nelson *Arm*?"

Briefly returning to Burnham Thorpe in 1787 he got married, but after only a short time he was again itching to return to the sea. However, despite writing numerous letters to the Admiralty he was ignored for nearly 5 years because there was no need of him in peacetime, until the eruption of the French Revolution, when the declaration of war with France brought him back to the Sea Lords' attention.

Nelson was recalled, and his career accelerated. Bravery, foolhardiness, and a desire to always prove himself to others, particularly his king and country, led to rapid promotion and the love of an adoring public. His career was often helped by the steady stream of self-praising letters he fired off to newspapers, and friends in high places constantly extolled his victories.

Emperor Napoleon had assumed command in France, and his armies terrorized Europe. In time England knew his attention would be turned to them, and only the English Channel and the British fleet could stand in his way. Nelson was vigilant, and as rear admiral he watched for the French fleet to emerge from their port. They slipped past him, however, and landed Napoleon and his army in Egypt, but Nelson had his revenge when he cornered the

French ships in Aboukor Bay on the Nile and destroyed them in a one-sided engagement.

During the battle he sustained a serious head wound, and his fleet put in to the port of Naples to get him some urgent treatment. While recovering there he fell in love with the teenage wife of an elderly English lord, Lady Emma Hamilton. This relationship endured until his death, and the doting 70-year-old lord actually accompanied them throughout the affair, seemingly oblivious, even when she gave birth to a daughter for Nelson, whom he called Horatia.

The English establishment deemed this flagrant debauchery while his wife waited dutifully at home, but it only hardened Nelson's contempt for his superiors and those he considered lesser seamen. A classic example occurred at the battle of Copenhagen when Nelson, as Number Two, was ordered to retreat by the flagship. Putting his telescope to his blind eye, he remarked that he was unable to see any such orders being flown, so he continued the attack and won a great victory. The overwhelming praise of the public prevented the Lords of the Admiralty from taking any action against him, although they were furious.

On his brief return to London, Nelson found himself still snubbed by the King and the establishment for his open sex life, but his public still adored him. With rumors of Napoleon's transport fleet being ready to sail from France, the whole country believed only one man could stop the upcoming invasion: Admiral Nelson.

Napoleon Bonaparte, knowing that to cross the treacherous 20-odd miles of the English Channel would be suicide unless his troops could be protected from the constantly roving British fleet, had rebuilt his navy. And with new Spanish allies, he looked to establish control of the oceans and conquer England. Ironically, however, the revolution that had brought him to power had also killed off most of his country's best naval officers.

In August 1805, saying goodbye to his beloved Emma and their daughter, Nelson boarded his flagship, the famous HMS *Victory*, and left England for the last time, knowing that the battle he was about to undertake would determine the fate of his country. Having his 47th birthday party with his fellow captains at sea, Nelson expounded on his plans to attack the French, under Admiral Villeneuve, using new and daring tactics. He planned to use two columns of ships in line to smash through the French fleet, isolate individual ships, and ultimately destroy them. He finished the meal by saying, "I've had the happiness to command a band of brothers," for that was how he had grown to view his fellow officers and the sailors under him.

On October 19 the French and Spanish fleet sailed from Cadíz and found the English ships shadowing them. Numbers favored the French—they had thirty-three ships of the line and seven frigates to England's twenty-seven major ships and four frigates—but Villeneuve was wary of the English admiral with the reputation of doing the unexpected and his well-trained sailors, who were the complete opposite of those in his own command.

Early on the morning of the October 21 Nelson made his move. At 4 A.M. he formed his ships into two lines, and at daybreak the French saw the English fleet, headed by Nelson's flagship the Victory, bearing straight toward them.

With little wind, progress was painfully slow, and Nelson took the time to write a will in his great cabin, witnessed by his reliable Number Two, Thomas Hardy. He left everything to Emma and their baby, Horatia, who along with the Navy were the only real loves he'd found in his life. Then he dressed for battle in his best uniform and went on deck. His captains begged him to move to a smaller, faster frigate where he would be safer and able to see more of the battle, but Nelson refused, wanting to be in the forefront of the coming action. He had even put on all his glittering medals and decorations, making him the most impressive target on the most impressive ship. Flying the message "England expects every man today to do his duty" from its rigging, the Victory bore on. At midday the fleets engaged, with the French firing first, then the British unleashing their broadsides as they cut through the French lines at almost walking pace.

Patrolling his deck, viewing every aspect of the battle, Nelson was shot by a sniper from the rigging of a French ship just after 1 P.M., the bullet passing through his shoulder and lungs, eventually severing his backbone and paralyzing him from the waist down. Grief-stricken officers carried him gently to his cabin. For another

2 hours the battle raged outside as Nelson writhed in agony below, until finally Hardy came and told him that some fifteen French ships had been sunk or captured, with no British losses. "Only fifteen?" asked Nelson, his lungs now filling with blood. (The figure later became twenty.) Reminding his doctor that his family must be looked after by the country, he succumbed to his wounds and died surrounded by weeping officers.

A mood of sadness swept the fleet as confirmation of his death spread, but he had saved England, as a bitter Napoleon realized his hopes of invasion were gone. He went on to meet another outstanding English general on his own day of reckoning at Waterloo.

Nelson was returned to England, his body ironically preserved in a cask of French brandy, to the biggest funeral the country had ever seen. Fifty streets were named after him in London alone, and more than 100,000 people paid their respects to his body in only 3 days. Horatio Nelson had written some years earlier, "A glorious death is to be envied."

MENUS

Fully stocked, HMS *Victory* carried approximately 4 months of supplies for some 900 men, although the diet of the common sailor consisted of 2 pounds of salted beef or pork and weevil-infested biscuits most days, washed down with either the 8 pints of weak beer or 2 pints of rum they were issued daily.

Nelson tried to give them fresh foods as often as possible. He was famous for the quality of the food served in his great cabin. The *Victory* carried many live animals for the admiral's table. Nelson and his officers ate breakfast together around 7 A.M., with tea, hot rolls, toast, and cold tongue. Then they concentrated on the ship's business until 2 P.M., when a band would began to play, announcing the end of their work for the day.

At 2:45 P.M., to the tune of "The Roast Beef of Olde England," it was announced that dinner was ready. The meal usually lasted for about 2 hours, always three courses, each with different wines, then the band played again as the officers strolled on deck taking liqueurs. Cakes, biscuits, and rum punch usually rounded the day off at about 8 P.M.

An invitation to Nelson's table was greatly anticipated by all the officers in his fleet, and although he ate sparingly himself, he knew that his famed hospitality was another way of maintaining the high morale of his captains.

Menu

Celery and Stilton Soup

"Dry Devils" Roast Pheasant
(dry with Seville orange sauce)

Asparagus in Crisp Rolls

New Potatoes and Spiced Hollandaise

Celery and Stilton Soup (6)

2 oz salted butter
4 tbsp plain flour
8 oz milk
1 pint clear unseasoned stock
8 oz coarsely grated Stilton
7 oz finely chopped celery
sea salt and black pepper

- Fry the celery lightly in the butter for 4 to 5 minutes. Stir in the plain flour and cook for another 2 minutes, stirring all the time with a wooden spoon.
- Add the stock and milk, cover, and simmer for about 12 minutes or until the celery is completely tender. Gradually add the grated Stilton and season to taste.
- Gently reheat to serving temperature; garnish with celery stalks and a spoon of sour cream.

Roast Pheasant with Orange Sauce and Simple Gravy (6)

3 or 4 young pheasants, plucked, cleaned, and hung for 3 to 4 days
3 oz salted butter
flour for dusting
8 strips streaky bacon
½ pint water or game stock
½ tsp sugar
6 oz dry sherry
salt and pepper
6 drops wine vinegar

- Preheat the oven to 420°F. Place 2 oz of the butter in a roasting tin and melt in the oven.
- Dust the birds lightly with flour and brown gently, breast down, in the butter until golden all over.
- Place the pheasants' breasts upwards and lay 2 strips of raw bacon across each. Roast for 35 to 40 minutes for medium rare, 10 minutes longer for well done.
- Remove from oven, put on tray, and allow to rest for 15 minutes before serving.
- Meanwhile, to make simple gravy, spoon off most of the surface fats from the roasting tin; this can be done on the stovetop. With a wooden spoon scrape the pan, using the scrapings for flavor. Now add the vinegar and game stock or water, and bring to a boil for about 2 minutes; add the sugar and the sherry, test, and season with salt and pepper to taste.
- This is a thin gravy, but you can reduce it for a few more minutes to thicken if you wish. Add remaining butter, strain into a sauceboat, and serve with watercress and fried breadcrumbs as a garnish.

Orange Sauce

- Put 1 cup orange juice, 1 cup water, and 1 cup sugar in a saucepan over medium heat. Add 4 tbsp cornstarch and stir until it begins to thicken. Add 1 cup currant jelly and 2 tbsp grated orange rind to finish.

Asparagus in Crisp Rolls (6)

1 lb thin asparagus, cleaned and peeled
6 oz heavy cream
2 large egg yolks
salt and pepper
½ tsp grated nutmeg
2 oz salted butter
5 oval-shaped crispy rolls

- Hold the asparagus between your fingers and bend slightly; there is a natural point at which it bends. Cut at that point, then discard the ends and cut the asparagus tips into 2-inch pieces. Cook in boiling salted water for 8 to 10 minutes or until tender. Drain, but save the water.
- Slice the rolls across the top, remove the insides, and lightly fry the lids and shells in butter.
- In another pan beat the cream with 4 tbsp asparagus water, the nutmeg, salt, and pepper. Beat the egg yolks in a dish, and gently add the cream mix to them to make a fine velvety sauce.
- Add the asparagus pieces to the sauce and spoon into the fried rolls.
- Replace the lids and serve either as a starter or a main course accompaniment.

New Potatoes and Spiced Hollandaise (6)

2–3 lb well-scrubbed new potatoes (don't peel)
½ tsp ground turmeric
2 egg yolks
6 oz unsalted, softened butter
1 clove peeled, crushed garlic
2 level tbsp plain yogurt
½ cup toasted almond slices

- Put the potatoes and the turmeric in boiling salted water and boil for 10 to 15 minutes until cooked; drain well.
- Place the egg yolks and garlic in a small pan over simmering water, whisk gently until the eggs start to thicken, and gradually add the softened butter until it's all blended. Do not overheat or the sauce may separate.
- To finish, add the yogurt with a touch of turmeric, stir for a few seconds, pour over the potatoes, and sprinkle with toasted almonds.

ABRAHAM LINCOLN
Washington, D.C.
April 14, 1865

We here highly resolve that these dead shall not have died
in vain; that this nation under God, shall have a new birth
of freedom; —and that the government of the people, by the
people, for the people, shall not perish from the earth.

—Abraham Lincoln, Gettysburg Address, November 19, 1863

The sixteenth president of the United States spoke these famous words as he dedicated the cemetery to the 40,000 dead of the Battle of Gettysburg, Pennsylvania, which had finally heralded the end of the American Civil War.

Abraham Lincoln was born in a small log cabin in Hardin, Kentucky, in 1809. A self-taught man of unusual strength and stature, he was renowned as a storyteller and a man of integrity. While working on cargo boats in New Orleans he educated himself to be a lawyer, qualifying in 1836.

Intensely interested in politics from the beginning, he joined the Illinois legislature in 1834 and ascended to the House of Representatives in Congress in 1847. A man of very fixed ideas and convictions, often against the advice of friends, he decided to make a run for the White House. He won the presidential campaign in 1860 mainly because the Democratic party was split. But many of the ideas on which he was expounding in the presidential debates with his rival, Stephen Douglas, induced seven of the southern slave states to secede before he even assumed office in March 1861. Unknowingly, he had set in motion the wheels of the American Civil War.

Immediately on taking control of the federal government, he decided to garrison Fort Sumter in North Carolina with troops from northern states, against the advice of his cabinet. The new troops were immediately surrounded by those of the fiercely independent southern state and then attacked on April 12, 1861.

Lincoln called for more volunteers to put down the Carolinians, at which point another four southern states announced they were leaving to join the new Confederacy. And so by June 1861, only 3 months after taking office, he had effectively split the country. Alabama, Arkansas, Florida, Georgia, Louisiana, Mississippi, North Carolina, South Carolina, Tennessee, Texas, and Virginia had set up a provisional government at Montgomery, Alabama. Jefferson Davis was named their president and had made his capital at Richmond, Virginia, now the head of the new Confederate States of America.

The Confederacy had some 5 million whites and more than 3 million black slaves. Slavery was a bone of contention for the righteous Lincoln, who in 1862 announced his Emancipation Proclamation, which was the beginning of the end of slavery in America.

This proclamation effectively changed the war from the initial fight against the secessionists to a moral fight against slavery. It also prevented the European powers of England and France from recognizing the Confederacy and kept them on the sidelines.

For the next 3 years the Civil War, in which the North held all the advantages with twice the manpower and all the major industries, raged. It eventually claimed more than 620,000 lives (360,000 Union and 260,000 Confederate), more than the combined American dead from all other wars between 1775 and 1975.

At the end of the conflict, President Lincoln had to use all his powers of noble oratory and personal integrity to control his vengeful cabinet as the war drew to a close. Many members of his cabinet wanted to treat the South harshly for their defection, but Lincoln insisted on reuniting the Union, even though reunification policies poisoned relations between North and South for more than a century after his death. Reelected as president in 1864, he sought to end this crippling fight and bring peace to the nation.

The South's most successful commander was General Robert E. Lee, who launched the Confederacy's second invasion of the North in 1863. His hopes were finally crushed at the battles of Gettysburg and Vicksburg, leading to his final surrender, and the end of the war at Appomattox on April 9, 1865. At last Lincoln could dream of peace for his presidency, a situation he had never experienced and never would.

Though popular with many of his compatriots, he was detested by others. One, a young southern Shakespearean actor named John Wilkes Booth, had gathered a group of dissidents together and in 1864 detailed plans to capture Lincoln, take him to Richmond, and ransom him for the large number of Confederate troops the North was holding, perhaps enabling the South to fight on a little longer with these badly needed reinforcements.

The kidnapping was to take place on March 17, 1865, when Lincoln was scheduled to attend a play at a hospital. However, the president changed his mind and the plot failed. In those days the president sometimes traveled with only one or two bodyguards.

With the ending of the war a few days later, Booth became even more furious when the president suggested in a speech that blacks should get certain voting rights. He decided that assassination was the only answer. Maybe with Lincoln's death the South would rise again. President Lincoln was constantly warned of various plots against him but ignored them all.

On April 14 Booth discovered that Lincoln would attend the theater that evening to watch a play, *Our American Cousin*. Quickly organizing his other conspirators to kill the vice president and the secretary of state the same night, he said he would take care of Lincoln personally.

Arriving at Ford's Theatre at 8:30 P.M. that night, after his Good Friday dinner, the president sat in his box with his wife and their friends Henry Rathbone and Clara Harris.

Booth went for a drink in a saloon outside, then made his way to the state box. The president's bodyguard, John Parker, had inexplicably left his post, and Booth was able to enter the box and shoot Lincoln in the back of the head at point-blank range.

A shocked Rathbone jumped at Booth, who slashed him with a hunting knife and then jumped 11 feet to the floor below, snapping his left ankle in the process. Flashing his knife at a stunned audience of more than 1,000 people who didn't understand what was happening, he made his way out of the theater by the back door, mounted his horse, and made off into the night.

The other plots had met mixed fates. The vice president escaped unharmed, and the secretary of state was stabbed but survived. Booth and another of his gang, David Herold, met up at the Garrett farm in Virginia but were finally tracked there by the authorities on the morning of April 26. Herold surrendered, but Booth refused and was eventually shot to death and had the barn burnt down around him.

Taken to the Petersen House across the street from the theater, President Lincoln never regained consciousness and was declared dead at 7:22 A.M. on April 15.

A presidency that came into being at the beginning of America's greatest war was ended just days after it finished.

MENUS

Last Meal in the White House

Clear Mock Turtle Soup (Using Oxtail)

Roast Virginia Fowl with Chestnut Stuffing

Baked Yams

Cauliflower with Cheese Sauce

Favorite Food

Chicken Fricassee

Dilled Chicken Fricassee (4)

⅓ cup all-purpose flour
1 tsp salt
½ tsp paprika
1 tbsp vegetable oil
4 bone-in chicken breast halves, skin removed
2 cups chicken broth
¼ cup fresh dill, chopped
8 small new potatoes, scrubbed
12 oz fresh asparagus, ends trimmed
1 tbsp lemon juice

- In a medium-sized bowl, mix the flour, salt, and paprika. Coat the chicken with the flour mixture, shaking off the excess. Reserve flour mixture.
- In a large, deep, nonstick skillet, heat the oil over medium heat.
- Add the chicken, meaty side down, and cook for 1½ minutes on each side or until well browned. Remove to a plate with a slotted spoon.

- Pour the broth into the flour mixture remaining in the bowl and whisk until smooth. Drain the fat from the skillet and wipe it clean.
- Add the chicken broth mixture and 2 tbsp dill. Stir to mix. Add the chicken meaty side up and the potatoes. Bring to a boil over high heat. Reduce the heat to low. Cover and simmer for 10 minutes.
- Lay the asparagus over the top. Cover and simmer for 15 to 20 minutes more, or until the chicken and vegetables are tender. Remove the pan from the heat. Stir in the lemon juice and the remaining 2 tbsp of dill. Serve hot.

Mock Turtle Soup

1 large onion, finely chopped
1 tbsp butter and 2 tbsp olive oil
2 lb meaty oxtails
1 garlic clove, mashed
3 whole cloves
¼ tsp thyme
1 bay leaf
¼ tsp allspice
1 tbsp flour
3 cups hot water
3 cups chicken stock
1 cup chopped peeled tomatoes
salt and pepper
½ thin-skinned lemon, chopped, rind and all
1 tbsp parsley
2 hard-boiled eggs
sherry

- Brown the onion in the butter and oil, add the oxtails, and brown slightly. Add the spices and herbs, then stir in the flour until it bubbles gently, adding more butter and oil as needed. Pour in the hot water and stock and bring to a boil.

- Add the remaining ingredients, except the egg and sherry. Simmer for 2 hours.
- Remove the oxtail, cut the meat and marrow away, and add back to the soup; discard the bones.
- When ready to serve, chop the eggs coarsely and stir into the soup. Ladle into bowls, stir a teaspoon of sherry into each, top with parsley, and put a cruet of sherry on the table—for atmosphere if nothing else.

Roast Virginia Fowl with Chestnut Stuffing

- To make the stuffing, take 2 cups dry breadcrumbs and mix in ½ cup chopped fresh chestnuts, 1 tsp chopped fresh sage, a pinch of poultry seasoning, 2 oz chopped onion, salt, and pepper. Work in 4 oz soft butter and enough chicken broth to help bind.
- Stuff into two large fowl, seasoned inside and out, and roast at 350°F for about 1 hour. Let rest for 10 minutes, then serve.

Baked Yams (2)

Yams are a wonderful, spleen-nourishing food, warming and orange in color, mildly sweet. Yams are also beneficial to the kidneys. This is comfort food at its simplest.

2 yams (my favorite are red jewel yams, but any will do)

- Preheat the oven to 450°F.
- Wash the yams thoroughly. Prick the skin three or four times with a fork and place them on a foil-lined baking sheet. Place in the heated oven and bake for 1 to 1½ hours until they are tender when pierced with a fork.
- Yams are delicious by themselves, but if you desire you may slice your cooked yams and add butter, salt, pepper, and nutmeg to taste. I eat them skin and all. It is advisable to cook extra; they are equally delicious at room temperature the next day.

Cauliflower with Cheese Sauce

1 large head of cauliflower, or florets
2 tbsp butter
1 tbsp flour
1 cup hot milk
salt and pepper to taste
¾ cup grated cheddar cheese
1 lemon

- Cook the whole cauliflower or florets in boiling water, salted, with 1 lemon, for 15 minutes. Drain.
- Blend butter and flour together, add hot milk, and boil until thick. Add seasonings and cheese; stir until cheese melts.
- Serve over the cooked cauliflower.

LEONIDAS, KING OF SPARTA
Thermopylae, Greece
August 18, 480 B.C.

Go tell the Spartans, stranger passing by, that
here, obedient to their laws, we lie.

—Simonides, memorial stone at the Thermopylae Pass today

In August 480 B.C. the Persian King Xerxes assembled the largest army the world had ever seen. Estimated at anywhere from 500,000 to 1 million men, it was brought together from more than twenty nations under his dominion with one aim: the destruction and subjugation of Greece, a persistent thorn in the Persian's side.

That he failed in his quest can be attributed solely to the courage of a warrior race that helped unite the fragmented Greek states of the day by their heroism and sacrifice at the site of one of history's greatest battles, Thermopylae.

Seeing the oncoming Persian hordes, the Greek states, always at odds with each other, could reach no consensus on what to do. Some sued for peace; others prepared to surrender or flee. One state refused to bend: the warrior nation of Sparta.

From childhood the Spartans were trained for war, enduring extraordinary conditions and hardships to forge a warrior race that terrified anyone who opposed them.

Their heavily armored infantry were trained to execute their orders fearlessly, without question. Their whole life was dedicated to the art of war. Weak children were left in the open to die at birth so the nation would have only the strongest warriors in their ranks.

With the Persian force getting closer, the Greeks squabbled constantly about what to do. The Spartans, under their two kings, decided to act. All Greece waited for a leader to follow, and many states even thought of joining Xerxes to save themselves.

Not the Spartans. Looking at the size of the opposing forces, they decided to create a holding action at the pass of Thermopylae, some 85 miles from Athens, an area the Persians must pass through. In theory, their huge numbers would be constrained by the narrowness of the pass, and the superior Spartan warriors could make them pay a heavy price and give the other Greek cities a chance to fully mobilize.

Thermopylae is a collection of sulfur springs and had long been the gateway to Greece and the scene of many earlier battles. Because of its rugged mountains and narrow passes, the Spartans believed that the Persians would not be able to use their superior numbers against them, and if the fight were between equally balanced forces, the Persians' morale could be seriously dented, changing the odds in the Greeks' favor in the battles that would surely follow.

Like all the other states in Greece, the Spartans consulted oracles and looked for the guidance of the gods in determining the opportune time for battle. This created great frustration for their two kings, who knew that any more delay would see Xerxes through the pass.

One of the kings, Leonidas, grew tired of waiting. Under Spartan law he could mobilize only his bodyguard of 300 elite troops to follow him. He elected to advance to Thermopylae, believing that when other states saw the Spartans committed to this war they would rally, put aside their differences, and fight as one Greece.

Before leaving Sparta, Leonidas informed his bodyguard that this would be a one-way mission. Sparta was going to make a stand that would rally the nation. There would be no return for any of them. The troops accepted this without flinching.

In Spartan life, a baby was deemed either fit to be a soldier or, if a girl, hardy enough to bear one. At the age of 7 the boys were taken into military academies and worked relentlessly. By the age of 20 they had spent all their growing years in training, sometimes naked, for days on end in hostile weather to become the hardened fighting machines that Leonidas now commanded.

Taking their Helots, who were personalized slaves trained to feed and support the warriors, the Spartans marched north. Along the route other states, seeing the Spartans committed to the cause, began to send their forces in support. The Spartan heavy infantry, carrying more than 60 pounds of body armor each, with red cloaks and 8-foot spears, was a fearsome sight as it ground relentlessly toward the pass of Thermopylae.

By the end of the 6-day march more than 7,000 support troops had rallied to Leonidas. Quickly securing the pass and repairing the fragile wall left over from other conflicts, the Spartans awaited the arrival of Xerxes.

Over the next few days the Persians, who were so sure of victory that they had made no effort to secure the pass, started to arrive on the plains outside. From Egypt, India, Assyria, Arabia, Babylon, Ethiopia, and many other subject nations, the mighty force took almost 2 days to assemble outside the entrance.

On August 18, 480 B.C., the first ranks of Persian troops began to mass outside the narrow pass. Leonidas decided to give the honor of facing the first attack to the Thebians, brave troops and strong fighters in their own right. Though only about 750 in number, they had a front line of seventy men, some ten ranks deep in front of the wall, and true to Leonidas's calculations the first Persian forces, the Medes, though many times their number, could face them only with the same numbers.

The Medes were like most of Xerxes' forces, lightly armored with wicker shields, used to using superior numbers and flanking maneuvers to crush their foes. In straightforward head-to-head conflict with the armored Thebians they stood little chance.

From his throne on a cliff top overlooking the battlefield, Xerxes saw a slaughter unfold before him as a wall of Persian dead was erected before his eyes. Only as the Greeks grew weary with the slaughter did the Medes hold their ground. And as the Greek troops began to tire against the enormous numbers facing them, Xerxes saw for the first time why the Spartans had such a fearsome reputation.

Like all Spartan kings, leading his troops from the middle of the first rank, Leonidas had his pipers sound the Thebian withdrawal. One second the Medes were engaged, the next they found themselves facing an empty patch of ground, at the end of which was a solid wall of metal advancing at a slow, measured tread toward them.

Making no sound and standing shoulder to shoulder, the superbly trained Spartan warriors cut through the Medes like butter, the piles of dead mounted even higher, and the Spartans drove remorselessly on until the Persians ran screaming from the pass.

Again and again that day the Persians threw different nations against the Greek lines. By the end of the afternoon they had to use whips to drive them on, such was the slaughter the Greeks inflicted on them. Leonidas continually placed fresh troops in front of them, with the Spartans always replacing weary troops and inflicting horrendous casualties on the increasingly terrified Persians.

After 7 hours, Xerxes finally decided to send in his elite troops, the 10,000 Immortals, handpicked sons of his generals and nobles, each one immaculately dressed in purple and gold. These proud troops were the cream of his empire.

When one died he was instantly replaced, hence the name *Immortal*. They made no difference. Seeing a chance to strike a heavy blow, Leonidas faced them with his Spartans, even though they had been fighting all day.

Xerxes was left fuming as his troops streamed in chaos from the pass, leaving more than 1,000 of their elite comrades behind.

After three more days of increasingly desperate fighting Xerxes was seeing his dream of Grecian conquest disappear before his eyes—until treachery came to his rescue.

A Greek farmer named Ephialtes informed him of a secret goat track that ran around the mountains and came out behind the Greeks. Sending his precious Immortals to follow Ephialtes over the mountains during the night, Xerxes knew for sure the Greeks would be defeated.

On hearing of his betrayal, and with the Persians only hours away from surrounding him, Leonidas sent all the other Greek troops to safety, telling them that the Spartans had vowed to fight to the end, and they would.

The other Greeks reluctantly left and went back to their home states to inspire everyone with the story of the Spartan bravery.

When the Immortals arrived behind Leonidas and his remaining troops that morning, Xerxes himself led the Persians in a golden chariot. It was a hollow victory. Even at the end the Spartans advanced and hacked into the Persian troops. Eventually, overwhelmed and chopped apart, the 300 Spartans lay dead around their king. More than 20,000 Persian troops died at Thermopylae; the spirit of their army was broken and never recovered.

The Greeks had been given the time they needed to mobilize. In the autumn and spring the Persian army and navy were crushed at the battles of Salamis and Plataea.

After the memory of what the 300 Spartans inflicted on them at Thermopylae, one can only imagine the effect on the Persian troops when they encountered the full Spartan army and more than 50,000 other troops at the battle of Plataea.

In defeat, Leonidas, King of Sparta, had sowed the seeds of the Greeks' eventual victory.

MENUS

Although the Spartans were famous for spurning the luxuries of other Greek states such as Athens, they used a slave system, which ensured that the warrior class was always well fed and cared for. All manner of fishes, rabbits, hares, olives, and breads were available to them. They disdained fancy sauces, but the harsh training regimens and the wars they fought necessitated eating lots of protein to ensure muscle growth.

The meat of kid and goat, little used in the West, is an exceptionally low-fat, easy-to-cook dish. The meat of the kid is bright pink with a light covering of thin white fat, and the best goat meat should be the same color.

Fire-Roasted Rabbit

1 rabbit, cleaned and skinned
6–8 slices bacon or pork
1½ tbsp fresh thyme
2 tbsp fresh oregano, chopped
4 tbsp black olive paste
1 tbsp chopped marjoram
3 tbsp extra virgin olive oil
1 tbsp lemon juice
4 finely chopped garlic cloves
sea salt and black pepper

- Make a marinade of the oil, juice, thyme, oregano, garlic, salt, and pepper. Rub all over the rabbit. Wrap the bacon around the rabbit and secure it with cocktail sticks.
- Roast over medium hot coals for about 30 to 35 minutes, basting with any remaining marinade.
- Before serving, sprinkle with marjoram and serve with the olive paste or a selection of olives and figs.

Whole Fish on the Fire (4)

2 whole fish, red snapper, red or gray mullet, or tilapia,
    preferably about 2 to 2½ lb each
juice of 3 fresh lemons
sea salt and black pepper
4 oz extra virgin olive oil
8 bay leaves
1 tsp chopped fresh oregano

- Score the fish diagonally at 2-inch intervals, rub the inside and
  outside with ½ the lemon juice, salt and pepper, and ½ the olive
  oil. Place 4 bay leaves inside each fish and sprinkle the oregano
  inside and out.
- Place the fish on a grill over hot coals and cook for about 10 to
  15 minutes each side.
- Sprinkle the remaining olive oil and lemon juice on the fish
  immediately before serving.
- Serve with a Greek salad.

Grilled Kid Chops

A deliciously simple recipe.

6 large chops from a young goat
3 tbsp extra virgin olive oil
1 bunch fresh chopped sage
1 clove chopped garlic
sea salt

- Rub the chops with oil, sage, garlic, and sea salt. Cover and rest
  for about an hour.
- Put on a medium grill and cook for about 3 to 4 minutes each
  side, turning only once.
- Serve with arugula salad, goat cheese, olive oil, and lemon juice
  dressing.

Grilled Fish with Pepper and Fennel Salad (4)

3 lb cleaned fresh sardines, with their heads on (clean them only
  if they are more than 4 inches long)
4 large chopped garlic cloves
4 tbsp extra virgin olive oil
4 tbsp coarsely chopped Italian parsley
lemon wedges
sea salt and coarse black pepper
3 tbsp white wine
juice of one lemon

- Place the sardines in a large shallow dish and cover with all the other ingredients except for the parsley. Turn them every 15 minutes for 1 hour; then drain and put them on a medium hot grill for about 3 minutes each side, or until they develop grill marks.
- Serve immediately with wedges of lemon and chopped parsley.
- Accompany with a salad of sliced red, green, and yellow peppers and sliced fennel, with an olive oil and lemon dressing.

Fruit with Yogurt and Honey

1 cup Greek yogurt
3 tbsp clear honey

- Combine, with a marble effect.
- For dipping, serve apples, pears, tangerines, grapes, figs, or strawberries.

CAPTAIN ERNST LEHMANN
The *Hindenburg*, Lakehurst, New Jersey
May 6, 1937

Get this, Charlie! It's fire, and it's crashing! It's crashing terrible! Oh my! Get out of the way, please! It's burning, bursting into flames and is falling on the mooring mast, and all the folks agree that this is terrible. This is the worst of the worst catastrophes in the world! Oh, it's crashing. . . . Oh, four or five hundred feet into the sky, and it's a terrific crash, Ladies and Gentlemen. There's smoke and there's flames now, and the flame is crashing to the ground, not quite to the mooring mast. . . . Oh, the humanity, and all the passengers screaming around here!

—Herbert Morrison, radio commentator,
WLS Chicago, May 6, 1937, 7:25 P.M.

On May 3, 1937, Captain Max Pruss ordered the Zeppelin airship *Hindenburg* out of its shed in Frankfurt, Germany, then shouted his customary "Schiff hoch!" ("Up ship!"). The well-trained ground crew released the mooring ropes and, giving it a symbolic push upward, watched the largest airship ever built soar into the sky. By his side in the central gondola the company representative, Captain Ernst Lehmann, checked his watch; it was 8:15 P.M.

The *Hindenburg* (LX129) was built the year before, in 1936. At 804 feet in length it was only 78 feet shorter than the *Titanic* and more than four times larger than the Goodyear blimps. In its first season to North and South America it had carried more than 2,800 passengers and was regularly turning away bookings. However, Nazi Germany was starting to take shape, and after its appearance at the Olympic Games with ominous-looking swastikas emblazoned on its tail fins, a certain frostiness had started to appear between the German and American governments.

The *Hindenburg* was originally designed to use nonflammable helium gas, which was available only in America, but remembering the use of airships by Germany as bombers over England in World War I, the Americans refused to supply the precious helium, and so it was forced to carry more than 7 million square feet of flammable hydrogen gas, a fact that helped close down the trans-Atlantic airship business in the coming days after more than 21 years of successful flights.

For about $720, passengers on the *Hindenburg* enjoyed a degree of luxury and personal attention that surpassed that of the great ocean liners of the day. There are many stories of passengers asking the crew when they were going to take off several hours into the flight, so smooth was its passage.

There were two decks for the seventy-two passengers, although on this trip it was carrying only thirty-six passengers and a crew of sixty-one.

Deck A, on the lower level, included the passengers' bedrooms (thirty-four double and four single berths), a reading and writing room that contained a baby grand piano made of aluminum and covered in antelope skin for lightness, and a spacious dining room. The sides of the lounge and dining room had sloping full-length windows, giving a majestic view of the countryside and oceans below. Normally traveling at an altitude of only 1,000 feet, the *Hindenburg* gave the passengers a clear view without any noise at all.

Deck B contained the toilets, the kitchen, crew quarters, a bar, and even a pressurized smoking room that had to be entered through an airtight door.

Shortly after midnight the *Hindenburg* entered a fierce storm over the North Sea, and Captain Pruss ascended over the clouds to about 2,100 feet to ride out the weather, then descended back to the regulation 1,000 feet at breakfast time. The passengers were constantly entertained. After breakfast bouillon was served at 11 A.M., checkers and cards were played, and drinks were served constantly. The hand-picked staff were chosen for their friendliness and efficiency, and Captain Lehmann often entertained the passengers with his prowess on the accordion. Tours of the ship were given twice a day, and the passengers marveled at the sophistication, power, and beauty of this engineering feat. There was even a ship's dog at the rear of the vessel.

The *Hindenburg* began to face strong headwinds on its way to the eastern seaboard, adding extra time to the trip and frustrating the officers, who prided themselves on their famous punctuality. However, the passengers were oblivious to any problems as the five chefs on board and the staff, under Chief Steward Kubis, attended to their every request.

At 3:07 P.M. on Thursday May 6, the *Hindenburg* arrived over New York City, showing its passengers the Empire State Building, the Bronx, and Central Park. A heavy storm began to hit its landing site at the Lakehurst Naval Air Station, and after consulting with the commanding officer, Charles Rosendahl, Captain Pruss decided to circle to the north for a while to await better landing conditions.

The hundreds of people who had gathered since early in the morning marveled at the size and grace of this airship as it turned around the Statue of Liberty; it was truly an awesome sign of the emerging power of Nazi Germany.

The passengers on board, being informed of the delay, merely shrugged and went for a long, leisurely lunch while looking out of the windows at the distant skyscrapers of New York.

At around 5 P.M. Captain Rosendahl sounded "zero hour," summoning the more than 200 ground support staff from their dry quarters to prepare for landing. However, Captain Pruss had drifted a little too far away when the airfield informed him that conditions were favorable for landing at 6:12 P.M. Shortly after 7 P.M. Rosendahl sent the airship its last message, "Conditions definitely improved, recommend earliest possible landing."

The *Hindenburg* was on its final approach, and events began to unfold rapidly.

At 7:07 P.M. it executed a sharp turn at full speed to the west at about 700 feet altitude.

At 7:11 P.M. it vented some hydrogen to bring its descent in line with the mast, awaiting docking.

At 7:12 P.M. the captain reduced the speed to idling and reversed engines to slow down; the altitude and speed were perfect, the crew were in their positions in the tail ready to release the rear landing wheels, and others had the tow ropes ready for dropping.

At 7:17 P.M. the *Hindenburg* dropped 2,400 pounds of water on the onlookers underneath as it trimmed its ballast and floated majestically to the docking tower.

Now only about 900 feet from the tower and 300 feet up, the crew dropped the first mooring rope, which was grasped by the eager ground staff.

The passengers and their waiting families were waving to each other when suddenly, at 7:25 P.M., witnesses saw a small flame appear in the rear tail section of the airship. Within seconds the ship was half consumed by a raging orange fireball. The passengers and crew had little time; many threw themselves through the windows to their death 300 feet below, but the airship hit the ground quickly, enabling some to stagger out of the inferno to safety.

Within 24 seconds the *Hindenburg* was completely consumed by flames. The horrific pictures and commentary by Herbert Morrison, the radioman who was reduced to tears watching it, were shown around the world the next day, effectively ending trans-Atlantic airship flight for years. Captain Lehmann, his clothes smoldering, was carried from the wreckage, saying over and over, "I can't believe it, I can't believe it." He died 2 days later from horrific burns, which covered more than 80 percent of his body.

It is incredible that only thirty-six people died (although many others had horrific injuries). To this day no definite conclusion has been reached on the causes of the tragedy.

Recent scientific tests have shown that the silver aluminum paint on the *Hindenburg* had the same flammable properties as solid rocket fuel. Others have speculated that lightning ignited the gas the airship released, others that sabotage had been used to discredit Nazi Germany.

The FBI released a 337-page investigation into the disaster, alleging that Lehmann himself set the explosion with a clockwork fire bomb as part of an elaborate plot to obtain helium from the United States. The bomb was supposedly set to go off when the airship was empty, but the 2-hour delay threw off the timing of the plot. We may never know. In any case, the days of the great airship adventure were over.

MENUS

On its last voyage, the *Hindenburg* carried 300 pounds of Beluga caviar, 220 pounds of fresh butter, 220 pounds of fresh fish, 800 eggs, 220 pounds of cheese and marmalade, and 55 gallons of mineral water, among other stores. Under Chef Xavier Maier, the *Hindenburg* represented the finest standards of service and presentation for one of the flagships of the new Germany.

Last Menu of the *Hindenburg*

Pâté à la Reine

Salad Carmen

Indian Swallow Nest Soup

Beef Broth with Marrow Dumplings

Pan-Fried Black Forest Trout

Cold Rhine Salmon with Potato Salad

Roast Gosling Meunière

Duckling Bavarian Style with Champagne Cabbage

Venison Beauval with Chateau Potatoes

Tenderloin Steak with Goose Liver Sauce, Chateau Potatoes

Pears Condé with Chocolate Sauce

Turkish Coffee, Cakes, Cheeses, Liqueurs

Captain Lehmann's Dinner, May 5, 1937

Pâté à la Reine

Fish in Black Butter

Duckling Bavarian Style

Venison Beauval

Chateau Potatoes, Champagne Cabbage

Pâté à la Reine

1 lb venison, trimmed weight
½ lb belly of pork, trimmed weight
½ lb chicken livers
1 small orange
1 lemon
2 garlic cloves
1½ tsp fresh thyme (more to taste)
1½ tsp whole and ground bay leaves
black pepper
salt
1 tbsp red wine vinegar
2 tbsp olive oil
½ cup red wine
1 tsp gelatin powder
a few kumquats to decorate

- Mince all three meats finely and put them in a bowl. Add the zest of orange and lemon, crushed garlic, thyme, olive oil, vinegar, a generous pinch of powdered bay leaves, and plenty of black pepper. Mix thoroughly and stir in wine. Cover and leave to marinate overnight.
- Season with salt; I find 1 tsp about right, but try a small nugget of the mixture to check. Turn the pâté into a terrine of about 2¼ pint capacity. Pack the mixture well down into the corners of the dish and use a spoon to hollow out slightly the center top. Cover with greaseproof paper and foil, and stand the dish in a roasting pan containing enough hot water to come halfway up the sides of the dish. Bake at 325°F for 2¼ to 2½ hours.
- Using a bulb baster, remove and reserve most of the juices that surround the pâté. Replace the greaseproof paper and foil, press the pâté lightly with 1½ to 2 lb weights, and cook for 1 to 1½ hours. Then drain off any remaining juices that have not been reabsorbed by the pâté. Mix all the venison juices that you have collected with the juice of the orange and measure.
- Add a splash of water if necessary to make ½ pint in total. Dissolve the gelatin powder in the mixture and use it to glaze the pâté, adding a few bay leaves and kumquats to decorate if desired.

Fish in Black Butter (4)

4 medium-sized trout, cleaned but with heads left on
salt and black pepper to taste
½ lb unsalted butter
4 tbsp fresh lemon juice
2 tsp small capers
2 tbsp coarsely chopped parsley

- Make sure that the fish is completely dry; season with salt and pepper inside and out.
- Place half the butter in a large frying pan and cook the trout for about 2 to 3 minutes each side. Remove from pan and place on heated serving dish.
- Put the remaining butter in the pan, heat until it becomes a nice golden color (don't burn it), add the lemon juice, capers, and parsley for 1 minute more.
- Spoon over the trout and serve immediately.

Venison Beauval (Brandied Venison Steaks) (4)

Venison is the meat of any antlered animal such as deer, elk, moose, or caribou.

4 loin steaks, about ¾-inch thick
2 lb butter
2 tbsp brandy
1 tbsp Worcestershire sauce

- Melt the butter over medium heat in a large frying pan. Quickly sear the steaks and cook on reduced heat for about 3 minutes each side.
- Mix the brandy and Worcestershire sauce and pour over steaks, simmer for about 1 minute, flame, and serve immediately.

Chateau Potatoes (6)

6 medium potatoes
2 tbsp unsalted butter
1 tbsp vegetable oil
1 tbsp finely chopped rosemary
½ tsp each of salt and pepper

- Peel potatoes. Using a paring knife, cut into 8-sided jewel shapes (alternatively, cut into thick, evenly shaped wedges).
- Place butter, oil, and rosemary in a large rimmed baking sheet.
- Set the pan in 425°F oven for 2 to 3 minutes or until butter is sizzling.
- Pat potatoes dry, place in heated pan, and stir to coat with butter mixture.
- Bake, stirring occasionally, 35 to 40 minutes or until potatoes are golden brown.
- Season with salt and pepper.

Baked Duck (8)

2 mallard ducks, cleaned
salt and pepper
1 large onion, chopped
2 ribs celery, chopped
4 slices bacon or salt pork
3 cups water
1 tsp prepared herb seasoning
2 chicken bouillon cubes

- Salt and pepper the ducks. Place in baking pan, add half of the onion and half of the celery, place other half in body cavities. Place the bacon, 2 slices per bird, across breast.
- Add water, herb seasoning, and bouillon cubes to pan. Cook at 300°F for 3 hours, basting every 30 minutes. Smaller ducks should cook 2 hours.
- When ducks have cooked, remove and wrap in aluminum foil to retain heat.

Duck Bavarian (4)

2 mallards, pintails, or black ducks, cleaned
¼ cup all-purpose flour
1 cup cooking sherry
1 cup cream

- Follow recipe for Baked Duck, then after ducks have baked, remove and pour pan drippings into saucepan. Bring to a boil, reduce heat to medium, add flour, and blend.
- Fold in sherry and cream. Remove from stove. Split ducks in half, place into baking pan, cover with sauce, baste, and heat for 5 minutes.

Champagne Cabbage (4)

1 large Savoy cabbage
½ bottle champagne (don't use a good one)
4 oz salted butter
salt and pepper
2 pints boiling water

- Remove outer leaves of cabbage, cut into four, then remove the core and shred finely.
- Put in colander and place over boiling water. Steam for 3 to 4 minutes and remove cabbage from steam.
- Place butter and champagne in large pan and heat gently. When butter and champagne are blended, whisk lightly, add cabbage, and season to taste. Serve immediately.

ELVIS AARON PRESLEY
Graceland, Memphis, Tennessee
August 16, 1977

Elvis Presley has left the building.

—Every concert promoter (Elvis never did encores)

On January 8, 1935, after 10 hours of labor, an exhausted Gladys Presley finally gave birth to the son she had always prayed for. As her husband, Vernon, rushed to her side, he saw the sadness on the doctor's face. The baby was stillborn. But his uncle put his hand on her stomach and said, "But Vernon, I think there's another baby in there." The doctor rushed back to her side. "He's right! There's a twin."

And so 30 minutes later, at 4:35 A.M., Elvis Aaron Presley was brought into the world. As his brother, Jesse Garon, was buried the next day in an unmarked grave in a cardboard box, the extraordinary life of the man who would always be called The King began in a dismal two-room shack in Tupelo, Mississippi.

From the beginning of his life Elvis was surrounded by music. His mother picked cotton during the day in the heat of the Mississippi sun, pulling her 1-year-old son behind her on a bundle of rags. Blacks and whites worked side by side in the cotton fields of the 1930s, and their singing and humming helped ease the burden of the long monotonous hours. In church every Sunday the choirs sang part gospel, part blues, and the young Elvis stood eagerly mouthing the music along with them.

When Elvis was 4, his father made him a guitar from an old cigar box, a broom handle, and some fishing line, and Elvis stood for hours belting out any tunes he could remember.

As his father drifted in and out of jail, Elvis grew even closer to his mother, who encouraged his musical leanings by taking him to different churches to hear other choirs. By the time he was 8 years old he was wandering through the town by himself, looking for anyone to sing a tune with. By 9 he had a repertoire of hill-billy songs and was hanging outside the local radio station (WELO) singing along to the sounds of his hero, Tupelo's "King of Country," Mississippi Slim.

As with many children in a broken marriage, the relationship with his mother shaped his life in many ways. As a child Elvis loved potato salad with his all-time favorite, deep-fried peanut butter and banana sandwiches as a main course. He hated fish and most vegetables, and his adoring mother made no attempt to change his eating habits. Double batter-fried chicken when available, meatloaf, and hamburgers were all Elvis ever knew, and although he was a lanky, lean teenager, the seeds of his eventual ill health were being sown.

At the age of 17, Elvis was nearly 6 feet tall, with sandy blond hair and heavy acne. He started dyeing his hair black at the age of 19, a look he kept forever, and as he started to make records and his fame grew, plastic surgery corrected the acne and all his teeth were capped.

Considered too risqué for mainstream America, with his gyrations and excessive body movements (they would film him only from the waist up on TV), his concerts sold out nonetheless. Hollywood signed him to do a stream of B movies, all based around Elvis getting the girl and singing his current hits. As he came under the control of manager Colonel Parker, his mother began to see her baby slipping away from her and so followed his father down the path of alcoholism, taking amphetamines and any other available pills to ease the pain of her life.

She and Elvis always used baby-talk to each other on their frequent phone calls when he was on the road, but unbeknown to him she was slipping fast. Finally admitted to Memphis Hospital on August 9, 1958 with severe cirrhosis of the liver, she died on August 14 at the age of only 46.

Elvis mourned his mother for days, blaming himself for leaving her and angry about the poverty she'd had to endure and about how, just when he could give her anything she wanted, she'd been taken away from him. This loss apparently created a scar that never healed.

He was unable to sleep, and the doctors gave him tranquilizer shots and the first of many sleeping pills to help get him through the traumatic days ahead. Those days became years.

Sobbing on her casket at the funeral, Elvis cried, "Goodbye darling, goodbye darling . . . lived my whole life for you, we'll keep the house, everything you loved, we won't change a thing."

Sick the next day, with a temperature of 102°F, Elvis received friends in his bedroom at Graceland, a habit that continued for the rest of his life, as he retreated into a world where he lived at night and slept all day.

With the passing of his mother, Elvis threw himself even further into his career. Gold record followed gold record, and the money and the women rolled in. He became more and more dependent on medication for his sleep and found no shortage of doctors and hangers-on to get him the pills he needed daily. Just as destructive as the drugs, his love affair with junk food continued unabated. His appetite was becoming legendary. At one sitting he ate eight deluxe cheeseburgers, two bacon, lettuce, and tomato sandwiches, and three chocolate shakes.

Over the years the excessive food and drugs caused major changes in his physical appearance. The Elvis who weighed only 170 pounds at age 20 was 75 pounds heavier 10 years later and still growing.

In 1974 a special medical team was installed in Graceland to help wean him off fat-laden pork chops, chicken-fried steaks, and the plates of cakes and cookies he could down effortlessly, all prepared for him by his loyal cooks.

Recommending a breakfast of two poached eggs, orange juice, and coffee to start the day right, the doctor was stunned to find

Elvis having his preferred breakfast of three double cheeseburgers, half a pound of fries, and a pound of bacon burnt to a crisp as a side dish.

Drastic dieting to prepare him for an upcoming movie or concert would help drop 20 pounds or more, but in a matter of weeks the weight would be replaced, usually with a little interest.

One particular night with pals, he had a craving for his favorite sandwich, "Fool's Gold Special," which was made of creamy peanut butter, grape jelly, and crisp lean bacon, piled inside a hollowed-out loaf sliced lengthwise and deep fried. A restaurant called the Colorado Gold Mine Company in the Rockies made it. Undeterred by the distance, he loaded his friends into his private plane and landed at Stapleton Airport after midnight, where the restaurant owner was waiting with twenty-two full sandwiches, a case of champagne, and a case of Perrier. Each sandwich contained more than 42,000 calories.

Elvis began to miss concert appearances, sometimes almost collapsing on stage, as his drug-filled body could not cope with the demands he placed on it. At the heart of everything was the terrible loneliness he'd felt since the death of his mother. Numerous women had passed through over the years, but with the exception of Priscilla Presley, whom he'd wooed when she was a 14-year-old girl in Germany and later married, none could fill the void he seemed to feel.

On May 28, 1977, while performing at the Philadelphia Spectrum, he couldn't remember the lyrics of his songs and was staggering about the stage. The next night, in Baltimore, his voice was so weak the audience couldn't hear him. He dropped the microphone, and eventually an assistant had to hold it for him.

It was his last set. He had taken more than 128 doses of drugs during the tour. His crew had discreetly started carrying oxygen tanks around in case they needed to revive him. On August 16 Elvis showed no signs of being ready to hit the road again. Normally he would go on a Jell-O diet to lose weight, or he would starve himself for days on end to fit into the only two jumpsuits he could wear. But as he climbed the stairs of Graceland with his girlfriend, Ginger Alden, on August 16, 1977, Elvis called down for some "ice cream and cookies, but not as much as usual," because he'd just finished eating spaghetti and meatballs.

As always, he was plagued by insomnia that night and took two packets of his prescription drugs, not mentioning to Ginger that he had codeine and morphine hidden in his huge bathroom along with numerous other medications.

After tossing about for a while he apparently still couldn't sleep, so he rolled away from the sleeping Ginger and went off to his bathroom. She woke just after 2 A.M., and seeing the bed empty and the light still on in his bathroom she went to look for him. There on the floor, on his knees, was the King of Rock 'n' Roll, Elvis Presley, dead at the age of 42.

The autopsy stated that he died of hypertensive heart disease. He weighed nearly 350 pounds at death, and it took five large men to lift him down the stairs to the hospital.

On August 18, 1977, with more than 4,500 floral tributes and tens of thousands of screaming mourners lining the streets, Elvis Aaron Presley was finally returned to his mother's side at Forest Hill Cemetery, Memphis, Tennessee.

A man who had everything—looks and talent, fame and money—could not cope with the loneliness within him. Each year more than 6 million fans pay homage to him at his Graceland home. The King lives on.

MENUS

Elvis Presley's last meal was a simple snack of frosted cookies and
ice cream, although a couple of hours earlier he ate spaghetti and
meatballs, one of his all-time favorites.

Favorite Foods

Fried Peanut Butter and Banana Sandwich

Ham Pancakes

Hawaiian Hamburgers

Baked Apple and Sweet Potato Pudding

Ham Bone Dumplings

The golden rule at Graceland, Elvis's home, was that breakfast,
his favorite meal, was to be served all day, except mornings.
Even the menu for his wedding to Priscilla on May 1, 1967, at
the Aladdin Hotel in Las Vegas, reflected Elvis's consuming love
affair with food.

Wedding Menu

Ham and Eggs

Southern Fried Chicken

Oysters Rockefeller

Roast Suckling Pig

Poached and Candied Salmon

Lobster

Eggs Minnette

Wedding Cake

Champagne

Spaghetti and Meatballs

1 lb spaghetti pasta
large pan boiling water, add salt

- Try to time the spaghetti so it is cooked at the same time as the sauce.

Meatballs:
2 lb ground beef
2 beaten eggs
1 chopped onion
4 tbsp Worcestershire sauce
¼ cup tomato ketchup
1 tsp oregano
salt and pepper to taste

- Lightly sauté onion in pan and then combine with all other ingredients and roll into golfball-size balls. Lightly brown meatballs in the frying pan and remove.
- Elvis liked a heavy tomato sauce with his meatballs, and if you use sauce from a jar, lightly heat sauce and put meatballs in to simmer for about 10 minutes; add six whole peeled tomatoes and about 1 cup of tomato juice.
- Put spaghetti in boiling water for allotted time, remove from heat, strain, and mix in large bowl with meatball sauce. Sprinkle with finely chopped oregano and Parmesan cheese and serve.

Fried Peanut Butter and Banana Sandwich (3)

½ cup creamy peanut butter
5 very soft bananas, mashed
12 slices white bread
4 oz soft butter

- Mix bananas and peanut butter together; make sandwiches and lightly fry in melted butter until golden brown on both sides.

Ham Pancakes (20)

1 cup regular pancake mix
½ cup cornmeal
1½ cups milk
1 beaten egg
2 tbsp melted butter
3 tbsp cream cheese
2 tbsp mayonnaise
1½ tbsp horseradish sauce
3 cups chopped ham, from hock or regular sliced

- In a large mixing bowl combine pancake mix, cornmeal, milk, egg, and butter.
- Pour a little batter on a hot griddle about 9 inches in diameter and fry the pancakes for about 2 minutes each side.
- In a separate mixing bowl mix the mayonnaise, cream cheese, and horseradish. Blend well.
- Add the ham, then spoon a little of the ham mixture on top of each pancake. Roll the pancakes and fasten with a toothpick.
- Place on a baking sheet and broil for about 2 minutes. Eat at once, with or without maple syrup.

Hawaiian Hamburgers

1 large can sliced pineapple, fresh if available
1½ lb lean ground beef
sea salt and ground black pepper to taste
4 hamburger rolls, poppyseed
2 tbsp pineapple juice, or use syrup from can
¼ cup light brown sugar
½ cup tomato ketchup

- In a mixing bowl season the meat with salt and pepper. Place a spoonful of the meat into the hole of each pineapple ring.
- In a separate bowl mix the ketchup, brown sugar, and pineapple juice, then mix with the meat.

- Shape into 4 patties. Grill or pan fry patties to required taste, fry or grill pineapple rings, then place a patty on one side of each bun. Top each with a pineapple ring and place other half of each bun on top.

Baked Apple and Sweet Potato Pudding

4 large sweet potatoes
4 medium-sized eating apples
1 cup water
½ cup light brown sugar
½ tsp cinnamon
½ tsp apple pie spice
½ cup melted butter
½ tsp vanilla essence
1 box graham cracker crumbs

- Wash and peel the sweet potatoes and apples, then cut into slices.
- Cover the bottom of the pie dish with graham cracker crumbs; layer the potato and apple slices over the top of the crumbs.
- Mix brown sugar and water and sprinkle over each layer. Season each layer with a sprinkling of apple spice, cinnamon, butter, and vanilla.
- Spread a handful of crumbs over the top of the pie and bake at 350°F for 45 minutes.
- Let stand for 4 to 5 minutes before serving.

Ham Bone Dumplings

1 large ham bone or leftover ham pieces
2 quarts water
salt and pepper

Dumplings:
2½ cups flour
1 tsp salt
½ cup vegetable shortening
1 cup cold water

- Simmer ham bone in water for 15 to 20 minutes. Season with salt and pepper.
- Combine dumpling ingredients to make dough. Place the dough on a floured board and roll very thin. Cut the dough into small pieces and drop into pot with ham. Cook for about 20 to 25 minutes.

LORD FREDERICK CHELMSFORD
Defeated at Isandlwana, South Africa
January 22, 1879

Who are these people, these Zulus that embarrass
our generals and convert our bishops?

—Benjamin Disraeli, prime minister
of England, to Parliament, 1879

As the nineteenth century wore on, the saying "The sun never sets on the British Empire" was born. In Australia, India, Africa, and throughout Europe and the Caribbean, the Union Jack flag was flown. Powered by the Industrial Revolution with aggressive merchant fleets and administrators backed up by the resolute forces of its army and navy, Great Britain ruled over more territory than had ever been conquered before by any other nation on Earth.

The "stand and fire" discipline of its army had prevailed over some of the mightiest forces in Europe, backed up by the latest artillery and cavalry with landed gentry in command. They could never have anticipated suffering their largest tactical reversal in more than 50 years against an enemy armed only with cowhide shields, short spears, and their own courage. They were about to meet the Zulus.

141

After arriving and anchoring themselves in the Cape Town region of South Africa for several years, the British had gradually moved east along the coastline until settling in Durban on the East Coast. More colonists were shipped over from England to further anchor the developments, and a bustling economy was swiftly developed.

The colonial administrator, Sir Bartle Frere, backed by his general, the heavily mustached Lord Frederick Chelmsford, was approached by Boer farmers descended from Dutch ancestry, with whom they would later have a major war, to defend them against the supposed threat of the Zulu king, Cetshwayo.

Seizing on this request as a way to acquire more land for the British Crown and advance their own political aims and careers, Bartle Frere and Chelmsford issued the Zulu king with an ultimatum they knew he could not agree to, which was the permanent disbandment of his armies within 30 days. The king instantly refused, as they knew he must.

And so on January 11, 1879, Lord Frederick Chelmsford led his forces, in three large columns, across the Buffalo River into Zululand. War was officially declared. In their eyes there could be only one outcome.

The Zulu king, Cetshwayo, ruled some 400,000 people with an iron fist, first killing his own brothers to secure the throne. He was the product of a military culture that had terrified all the other African tribes with whom they came into contact. The Zulu social system was built around its army, and from childhood the boys were groomed in large military camps to endure hardship and to sacrifice all for the benefit of their king. Marriage was not allowed until they had proven themselves in battle, and competition between their regiments, Impis, was extremely fierce as everyone vied for the king's approval and the right to marry.

Although he had an army of more than 40,000 fierce warriors, Cetshwayo was no fool. He had watched the British move along the coast for the preceding years, and he was content to rule in his own little kingdom, which surely contained nothing the white men would want.

However, the whole Zulu culture was founded on its military system. To disband the army was to disband his nation, so as the imperial troops crossed the river, Cetshwayo sat in his capital, Ulundi, with his Impis, pondering his next move.

Placing himself in charge of the central column of 4,709 troops, 302 wagons and carts, and more than 1,500 transport oxen, Lord Chelmsford, a society soldier with no real military background, was sure of an easy victory. Though warned by South Africans such as Paul Kruger about the Zulu army's ability to run all day across mountain tops and chew their cowhide shields for food, Chelmsford scoffed at how "undisciplined blacks" with no supply lines could stand up to his well-trained forces containing artillery, cavalry, and even rockets, with a solid bedrock of British soldiers equipped with the latest Martini–Henry repeating rifles.

As the columns moved north, dragging their carts and artillery in unseasonably heavy rains over the gentle hills of Zululand, Chelmsford's purpose in splitting his forces into three was to bring the Zulu army to battle with any one of the three powerful groups and smash it with one decisive blow.

Unknown to him, that thinking was mirrored by King Cetshwayo. Sending several thousand troops to harass the flanking columns as his feints, he sent the main body of his army south toward Chelmsford's main column with specific instructions to "crush the head of the snake."

By January 20, moving slowly by their standards to conserve energy, some 25,000 Zulus arrived undetected only 15 miles from where Chelmsford had set up his first base camp at a rocky outcrop on a plain dominated by a large dome-shaped rock called Isandlwana.

After first splitting his forces into three, Chelmsford made the first major mistake of the war: He split them again.

Acting on a tip from scouts who claimed they had seen Zulus to the north, Chelmsford moved half his troops at 2 A.M. on January 22, planning to take the Zulus by surprise and end the war with one blow.

With horse hooves and cartwheels muffled to avoid any noise, his troops marched through the night looking for the Zulu army, supposedly southwest of Siphezi. Incredibly, the Zulu warriors crossed his front without any detection, moving northwest to the unsuspecting camp at Isandlwana.

After searching fruitlessly for hours for his dream battle, a frustrated Lord Chelmsford elected to have lunch with his officers at the

Mangeni Gorge, leaving instructions not to be disturbed. As native porters lit fires and polished the regimental silver he loved to use, some 9 miles to his rear the Zulu army was preparing to inflict the greatest tactical defeat on the British Army in more than 50 years.

For many of the officers traveling with Lord Chelmsford, the expedition so far had been little more than a picnic, riding off during the day to hunt Zululand's abundant wildlife and then eating it in the evening while sipping the glorious wines they had brought with them.

However, keeping favor with the irritable lord meant not questioning any tactic or decision he made. Chelmsford hated to see his officers think for themselves. One of these thinkers was a General Anthony Durnford, who was in charge of the mounted native auxiliaries, and he was deliberately left behind at the Buffalo River, where he couldn't play a role in the battles to come. But Chelmsford had second thoughts and later ordered him to Isandlwana so he could keep more of an eye on him. On the morning of January 22 the veteran officer, who had the greatest respect for the Zulu nation, arrived with his cavalry at the base.

Riding into camp, the one-armed general saw the British troops under Henry Pulleine, in a relaxed mood, all believing Chelmsford was winning the war for them away to the north. Immediately the experienced Durnford sensed something was not quite right.

Following his uneasy feeling, he decided to send his mounted troops out in a screen around the camp. The second troop, under lieutenants Law and Roberts, spotted some Zulu boys driving cattle about 5 miles away from the camp. They gave chase, and as the boys disappeared over a ridge they followed them at top speed. Cresting the ridge, they froze in their tracks. Squatting quietly in a valley below them were some 25,000 Zulu warriors. They had found the army they were looking for.

On seeing the imperial troops, the Zulus rose as one and started to flow toward them without any apparent orders; the attack on the camp was about to begin. Chelmsford would have his decisive encounter, but not the result he envisaged.

Without any apparent communication and showing a terrific understanding of the British weaknesses allied with complete mastery of the terrain, the Zulu army, running at top speed, quickly formed the classic bullshead Zulu formation, with two horns of 5,000 warriors each running off to the flanks to encircle the camp. The head of the bull, some 15,000 strong, advanced straight on at high speed.

So fast was their deployment that the retreating troopers, on horseback, were able to give the camp only a couple minutes' warning. Surveying the coming onslaught, Pulleine still felt confident. He had more than 800 crack British troops who were already calmly forming familiar lines to deploy their devastating volley fire. Another 800 well-trained auxiliary troops were forming up around them. As his artillery began to fire he felt even more reassurance and security.

As the troops began to fire volley after volley at the advancing Impis, with rockets screaming through the clear blue sky along with the roar of cannons, he soon saw his confidence had been misplaced. The Zulu force, armed only with short stabbing spears (assegais) and shields, kept coming on, and the stretched British lines were beginning to waver.

By mid-afternoon it was all over. More than 1,500 imperial troops lay slaughtered, scattered over the plain; only a handful on horseback finally escaped. Generals Pulleine and Durnford lay together like brothers, stripped like all their men, with their stomachs slashed open to release their spirits to the heavens.

Meanwhile, Chelmsford's lunch had been disturbed by the rumors of smoke from the direction of the camp. Begrudgingly he sent one of his junior officers to look through a telescope from a small hill. The officer returned to report that he could see nothing significant. Lunch continued.

Later that day, a stunned Chelmsford returned to camp and witnessed an incredible sight: Hundreds of horses, oxen, and cattle lay dead, intermingled with more than 1,500 of his finest troops. Surely by now all the British territories in the south were under attack by the Zulus? He was forced to retreat and regroup.

However, the Impis had only returned to their king to sing his praises. He had had no intention to invade British territories; their job was done.

Another 10,000 troops were quickly dispatched from Britain, and they eventually got the victory they wanted at the battle of Ulundi. The Zulu power was broken and its king defeated, but even today in modern society their military traditions and strengths live on, defeated but not conquered.

MENUS

Chelmsford's Brunch, January 22, 1879

Although today much of the wildlife that used to exist in the whole of southern Africa is limited, particularly in Zululand, to reserves such as Pinda Mountain Lodge, in the nineteenth century the region was full of game. In fact, most of the shooting done in the first few days of the war was by British officers bringing food to the camp or trophies to be stuffed and shipped home later.

Lord Frederick Chelmsford, like all British gentry on campaign, insisted on a standard, so as his wagons carried all the accoutrements of war, they also carried regimental silver and a quartermaster and native servants trained to produce all the luxuries of home, even in the bush.

Eggs in the Bush (4)

I have fallen into the trap more than once of having someone in South Africa ask me, "One egg or two?" I'm a big guy, so I say, "Two," at which point two ostrich eggs are broken into the pan in front of me (equivalent to 16 large eggs). These were available to Lord Chelmsford but probably will not be in your supermarket.

  1 ostrich egg or 8 regular eggs
  ½ lb smoked snook, herring, snapper,
    or fresh salmon, shredded
  ½ cup fresh milk
  4 peeled, seeded, chopped tomatoes
  ½ tsp chopped sage
  ½ finely chopped onion
  ¼ lb unsalted butter

- Whip eggs; add a little black pepper. Avoid salt, as most fish will compensate. Add milk.
- Heat butter in nonstick pan and stir in the egg mixture, using a wooden spoon to stir constantly; keep the eggs moving so they make tighter clumps.
- When the eggs are almost cooked, add the onion, tomatoes, sage, and fish and serve on toasted brown bread with champagne and orange juice (mimosas).

Grilled Antelope Steaks

Antelope is a great substitute for beef and is a very lean meat. When cooking antelope, gazelle, springbok, or warthog you need to use even more oil in your recipes. In 1850 the standard oil of the British Army was a margarine made of suet, milk, and water. For this recipe, treat yourself and use extra virgin olive oil.

Lean flanks of antelope (venison, deer) marinated in oil, rosemary, and sage for at least 3 hours.

- Place on medium grill for 45 minutes (about 20 minutes each side), turning only once. Slice thinly.
- Serve with claret, Beaujolais, or Fleur du Cap.

Liver and Bacon
(Gazelle, Antelope, Springbok, or Veal) (4)

Although it may not be readily available at your local supermarket, liver of antelope, gazelle, and springbok, lightly floured, with chopped sage, makes a wonderful lunch. Possibly the nearest taste available for urbanites is veal or calves' liver.

2 lb calves' liver, thinly sliced
½ oz chopped fresh sage
¼ cup whole wheat flour
2 red onions, finely sliced
16 slices lean bacon
4 oz butter
salt and pepper to taste

- Heat pan with butter.
- Rub chopped sage into flour, add salt and pepper, and brush both sides of the meat.
- Place in pan with a little butter, sauté for 2 minutes each side. In separate pan place a little butter, onions, and a touch of sage. Grill bacon.
- Place liver on plate, with grilled bacon on top and onions to finish. Serve with fresh sliced pears and apples. Excellent with Fleur du Cap or any other fine Cape red wine or Pinotage.

Baby Sweet Pineapple with Salted Ham (4)

In Zululand there is a small sweet pineapple that grows wild, excellent grilled, eaten raw, or in salads. Much of the ham eaten in the Zulu wars was imported in cans from the United Kingdom, so the pigs and hogs in South Africa were particularly attractive to the officers.

1 pint maple syrup or honey
2 baby pineapples
2 lb ham steaks, gammon, wild pig, or hog
½ lb unsalted butter

- Cut ends off pineapples, retain for decoration. Heat pan, place half of butter in pan, then put the ham steaks in.
- In a separate pan place rest of butter and maple syrup.
- Cook ham steaks on both sides and place on a bed of pineapple leaves.
- Meanwhile, gently heat the syrup and butter.
- Slice baby pineapples thinly; place over the top of the ham with the syrup and butter sauce.

Squash (4)

An abundant, readily available food in southern Africa in the nineteenth century. For this recipe, try one of the many varieties, such as acorn squash.

1 medium-sized squash
3 cups apple sauce
6 oz butter
6 tbsp maple syrup
2 tbsp powdered nutmeg

- Cut squash in half lengthways (horizontally). Scoop out the inside seeds, then place in a baking dish and pour boiling water up to 1½ inches deep around them.
- Mix the other ingredients and place in the hollow squash.
- Cover with foil and bake for about 35 to 40 minutes at 350°F.

GAIUS JULIUS CAESAR
The Curia, Rome
March 15, 44 B.C.

Veni, vidi, vici. [I came, I saw, I conquered.]

—Julius Caesar

Born into a patrician Roman family in 102 B.C., Julius Caesar was schooled to be a military man from an early age. Although he grew up in a dynasty that had everything, he spent his youth austerely, as he was made a priest of Jupiter while still a child. He was forbidden any delicacies or real luxuries, habits that he kept for many of his campaigning years, eating little as an officer and banning wine for his subordinates.

In the Roman military Caesar was adored by his men from the beginning; he never asked anything of them in battle he wouldn't do himself. He often marched at the head of his troops, always coaxing more effort from them. The Rome of his day was full of jealous politicians, always squabbling among themselves for even more power. Rising stars such as Caesar were often sent overseas as consuls of legions to difficult places in the hope they might not return or, better still, their power would be dissipated by some loss on the battlefield, an unacceptable fate for a Roman general.

Caesar would not be denied what he considered his due. After serving successfully in the East for many years, in 58 B.C. he was given the giant task of subduing the Gauls, a fierce Celtic warrior race that was spread across France and Belgium. With up to 1 million fierce barbarian troops at their disposal, the Celts were determined to remain free, and therefore they were the greatest threat to Roman power.

From 58 to 51 B.C., Caesar launched a brilliant series of battles and sieges. His legions were often outnumbered by as many as eight to one. He systematically ground the tribes down with defeat after defeat until he eventually led their King Vercingetorix back to Rome in chains, for a glorious triumph at the head of his seasoned troops, who under Caesar had become Rome's finest available legions.

Installed as governor of Gaul, he started to reveal his other brilliant skills, using his powers of oration to finally unite the defeated tribes under Roman law, building many new roads to open up the region to Roman commerce, and imposing on everyone the Pax Romana, or Roman Peace.

Two brief invasions of Britain along the way had convinced him that the wet, miserable little island nation, with little known mineral wealth, was not really worth his time, so he began to turn his eye back to Italy and the political stage.

As his star grew, so did his enemies in the Senate, although they remained quiet out of fear of him. He formed Rome's First Triumvirate with two other generals, Marcus Crassus and the great Pompey, who had rid the Mediterranean Sea of pirates in a little more than 40 days, enabling Rome's commercial power to expand even more. Pompey further increased Rome's influence in the East, but his exploits were mainly ignored by the crowds in Rome, who followed and celebrated only Caesar's frequent victories.

Even more desperate to establish himself, Crassus went to Syria, where he conducted an abysmal campaign against the Parthians at Carrhal in Mesopotamia and was eventually murdered by the Parthian generals in a humiliating defeat for Rome. This left a frustrated Pompey all alone, facing a popular Caesar who now wanted to come home to Rome. Pompey forced the Senate to insist that Caesar disband his legions first, a motion that Caesar refused, knowing his troops were Rome's finest legions and his power base. But history dictated that no Roman general had ever led troops on Rome or could be permitted to.

In 49 B.C. Caesar and his veteran legions crossed the Rubicon River, which was at that time the border between Italy and France. As he crossed that small stream he knew that there was no turning back; there could be only victory or defeat now, as civil war was imminent.

Watching Caesar and his army march toward Rome, Pompey and all his followers fled to Greece to enlist the help of disgruntled eastern kings tired of paying yearly tribute to Rome, believing they would help tip the balance. But despite compiling a large army, they were wiped out by the pursuing Caesar at the battle of Pharsalus in 49 B.C., where once again the military genius of Caesar vanquished superior numbers.

Pompey fled the battlefield in desperation and looked to find some shelter in Egypt. Caesar followed not just to quash any more rebellion but also to extend the hand of peace to Pompey, who had been his friend for many years. He was horrified to be given the head of Pompey in Alexandria by Ptolemy XIII, the boy Pharaoh of Egypt, who was controlled by the palace eunuchs. Switching his attention to Ptolemy's sister Cleopatra, who seduced him at their first meeting, Caesar made Cleopatra the sole Pharaoh of Egypt, and after several months he destroyed the forces of Ptolemy and won over the people of Alexandria and eventually Egypt by his gracious treatment of them.

With Egypt now under his sway and no real military opposition to him anywhere in the Roman world, Caesar relaxed in Alexandria and conducted a heady love affair with Cleopatra, who quickly bore him his only son, Caesarion.

Life as a military man had bred simple tastes in Caesar, a tall, lean, handsome man with piercing blue eyes. He ate the food of the common soldier: bread, olive oil, porridge, and bacon. He held a form of epilepsy at bay with a fruit juice cocktail every day and, though surrounded by the gastronomic delights of the royal palace, kept his frame lean and hard, and he expected the same from his subordinates.

Although he was incredibly talented in many fields, Caesar's legions saw him as one of them. This connection with the real power of Rome, the army, caused endless frustration for the powerful, decadent senators, who for many years had taken the rewards and basked in the splendors of the treasures and land won by the troops.

On returning to Rome, Caesar launched himself into a rapid reform of the political system. Senators had to report to the Senate or lose their privileges, a novel idea. The legions were to be given good land to farm when they left the ranks; the calendar was revised, giving us the 365-day year we use today; and he handed more power in the running of the empire to the common man, the plebian.

An adoring Cleopatra followed Caesar to Rome, where, although she had his love, she endured the hatred of Calpurnia, his wife in a loveless marriage he had entered into some years before.

Seeing "the Egyptian harlot" who had stolen the heart of the most powerful man in Rome, a group of twenty-three senators, organized by Gaius Trebonius, decided their only hope of holding onto any remaining power was to kill Caesar because soon, three days after the Ides of March (March 15), he was leaving Rome to conduct another campaign against the Parthian nation.

On the night of March 14 Caesar attended a dinner party at the house of Marcus Lepidus with ten other senators. As usual, Caesar worked through the meal, dictating orders for troop movements and reform to an endless procession of scribes while managing to be polite and cheerful to his dinner companions.

Rising early the next morning at the home of his wife, he had his usual breakfast of crusty bread and olive oil with lemon juice and honey, and despite the pleas of Calpurnia, who wanted him to stay at home, he marched off to the Curia to meet the Senate, disdaining a bodyguard and chatting jovially to all he encountered on the way.

Seating himself on his chair in the Senate and bringing out his scrolls, he started to dictate more edicts to his team of scribes.

Not noticing the approaching group of senators, he worked on, and only when the first dagger penetrated his back did he attempt to rise. Apparently making no sound at all, he remained on his feet as all twenty-three rogue senators stabbed him, each one encouraging the others.

As the last dagger pierced his heart he finally fell, pulling his toga over his face as if to hide his pain. The shocked senators, suddenly realizing the horror of what they had done, panicked and raced away.

As news of his murder swept the city, it was obvious to the plotters that they had badly underestimated the power of Julius Caesar and the love the people had for him. They were all eventually destroyed by the wrath of the people and his loyal avenging legions.

But nothing could undo the tragic death of one of the greatest generals and leaders in world history.

MENUS

Although Caesar retained many of his old habits from his legion days, rising every morning to a breakfast of crusty bread, olive oil, lemon juice, and honey, like all wealthy Romans he indulged in a variety of foods brought from around the empire. Many Romans had their own fishponds in their home, keeping a variety of freshwater and saltwater fish readily available. Specially built aviaries ensured a constant supply of fowls at hand. Spices from Asia, oysters from Britain, and a never-ending procession of exotic game from Africa supplemented the tables of the rich. Most of the food was prepared so it could be eaten by hand, as the Romans shunned the use of forks and ate reclining on couches, while slaves hovered around with finger bowls to wash their hands and keep the food and drink flowing.

Dinner at the house of Marcus Lepidus, on March 14, 44 B.C., was kept simple because Caesar was intent on working through it, preparing for his upcoming campaign, while socializing with the eleven senators.

Caesar's Last Supper

Scillas (Big Shrimps)

1 lb lightly poached and cleaned big shrimps
1 tsp green pepper, ground
1 tsp chopped celery
½ tsp celery seeds
2–3 tbsp malt vinegar
6 tbsp liquamen, or fish sauce
5 hard-boiled eggs, chopped

- Combine all ingredients and chill for several hours.
- Serve on a bed of lettuce and garnish with pine kernels and radishes.

In Mitulus (Sea Mussels) (4)

3 lb fresh sea mussels
1½ tbsp liquamen, or fish sauce
2 large leeks, chopped
1½ tsp cumin powder
300 ml passum or ½ bottle Chardonnay
4 tsp black pepper
3 cups water

- Clean the mussels thoroughly.
- Mix all the other ingredients and cook gently as a broth for about 8 to 10 minutes.
- Add mussels last, cover, and simmer gently until mussels start to open.
- Serve immediately.

Aliter Baedinam Sive Agninam Excaldatam (Steamed Lamb)

12 large lamb cutlets
⅔ bottle Soave or dry Italian wine
2 large white onions, diced
2 tsp ground coriander, fresh if possible
⅔ cup liquamen, or fish sauce
1 tsp ground cumin
1 tsp chopped celery
2 tsp oil

- Seal the cutlets gently on both sides in a frying pan. Put the cutlets in a large pot with the onion, celery, and spices. Add liquamen, oil, and wine. Cover and then cook gently for 40 to 50 minutes.
- Remove the cutlets, thicken the sauce with a little cornstarch, and after letting the cutlets rest for 3 to 4 minutes, place on a tray and cover with sauce. Serve with plums, figs, and fresh rosemary for garnish.

Fabraciar Virides et Baianae
(Green and Baian Beans)

1 lb green beans, lightly blanched
½ tsp sea salt
8 oz dry white wine
1½ tbsp extra virgin olive oil
1 tbsp chopped fresh coriander
1 tsp cumin seeds
1 leek, finely chopped

- Place oil in a large frying pan, then add the leek and coriander; cook gently for 2 to 3 minutes.
- Add the wine, salt, and spices with beans. Toss and serve.

Pullum Frontonianum (Frontier Chicken) (4)

1 large (4 lb) chicken, cut into eight pieces
½ cup extra virgin olive oil
1 cup liquamen, or fish sauce
1 large leek, chopped
1 bunch fresh dill, chopped
1 tsp Indian red pepper
½ cup fig paste or syrup

- Seal chicken pieces in a frying pan until lightly golden on both sides. Remove from pan, mix with all the other ingredients except figs, and cook for about 1 hour in an oven at 400°F.
- Smear the fig paste on the plates, put chicken on top, sprinkle with red or black pepper, and serve.
- Garnish with bunches of fresh dill, hard-boiled eggs, and radishes.

Dessert Ambrosia

2 pints heavy cream
2 lb pulped fresh strawberries
3 egg yolks
3 egg whites, beaten stiffly

- Whip cream until it gets body, then add egg yolks; fold in egg whites and strawberries, place in a mold, and chill for 2 hours.
- Serve with single cream, sliced apples, and pears.

GEORGE ARMSTRONG CUSTER
Little Bighorn
June 25, 1876

Custer of the golden locks, his broad sombrero turned up over his hard browned face. The ends of his crimson cravat floating over his shoulders, and gold galore spangling his jacket sleeves. A pistol in his boot, dangling spurs on his heels and a ponderous claymore swinging at his side. A wild dare-devil of a General and a prince of advance guards, quick to see and act . . . he died as he lived, fighting his hardest at the head of his men.

—Obituary, *New York Tribune*, July 7, 1876

On May 17, 1876, the Seventh U.S. Cavalry Regiment rode out of Fort Abraham Lincoln, Dakota, in what would be for many of them the last time. At its head was one of the most colorful and controversial soldiers in American history, Lieutenant Colonel George Armstrong Custer.

Finishing thirty-fourth out of a class of thirty-four at West Point Military Academy, Custer was court-martialed for the first time within days of graduation but eventually saved from punishment by the beginning of the American Civil War and the Union's urgent need for officers of any type, a luck that followed him for many years.

He was flamboyant and headstrong from the outset of his career, and Custer's aggressive battlefield forays quickly endeared him to an enraptured public, but he was detested by many of the men in his commands for his recklessness with their lives in battle and harsh treatment in peacetime, while he himself often rode off to engage in his favorite pastimes, hunting and carousing with his wife, Elizabeth Bacon.

His superiors loved Custer, though, and admired the dashing young officer who would take all manner of risks to win battles, always emerging as the victor, with large numbers of enemy prisoners, guns, and artillery. They never paid much attention to the fact that he lost more troops in battle than any other Union general in the Civil War.

Six feet tall with broad shoulders, blue eyes, and long golden hair, Custer could do no wrong in the eyes of his public. Receiving the South's white flag of surrender at Appomattox from General Lee himself, Custer and his new wife, Elizabeth Bacon, set their eyes on furthering his career in politics, believing that the "Golden General" could one day aspire to the White House.

The end of the Civil War brought an end to glory and headlines. He was assigned to Texas at the head of the cavalry, and boredom set in. He frequently left his troops to have fun with his wife, while having any other deserters shot on the spot, without a hearing.

Eventually he went too far and was charged and convicted with abandoning his command. But General Philip Sheridan, who saw Custer as the perfect man to lead a campaign against the Cheyenne in Oklahoma, overturned his punishment.

Once more marching his men forward without proper intelligence or planning, Custer attacked the Cheyenne camp at Washita on November 27, 1868.

The warriors were absent hunting, but this didn't stop a frustrated Custer. The Seventh Cavalry attacked, slaughtering 103 women and children and more than 800 animals and burning all the Cheyennes' possessions. Again the public saluted their hero, but once again, they were never given the real facts of the "victory."

Apart from the massacre of the helpless, Custer had allowed a detachment of his soldiers, under Major Joel Elliot, to look for the missing warriors by riding east of the village. Elliot finally found them and was promptly massacred with all his troops.

Returning to camp to celebrate his victory, Custer completely ignored his missing cavalry. When their remains were finally discovered 2 weeks later, no one dared question what had happened to them. They were written off as casualties of the battle.

In 1873 and 1874 he had several small skirmishes with the Lakota Sioux in North Dakota. His take-no-prisoners attitude against the Indians hardened their hatred of the white men even more and sowed the seeds for his eventual destruction. His wife, Elizabeth, both before and after his death, saw herself more as his agent, constantly promoting him as a statesman, patron of the arts, or military genius.

With her prompting, he went to Washington in March 1876 and testified against the secretary of war over alleged corruption. This move seemed to backfire on him as a furious President Grant relieved Custer of his command on May 2. But once again the public came to his rescue, forcing the president to revoke his decision on May 8, sending him out West once more to meet his destiny at Little Bighorn. Custer had demanded to lead his beloved Seventh in what everyone believed would be the final confrontation with the Indians.

Leaving Fort Abraham Lincoln on the morning of May 17, Custer was part of a column commanded by Brigadier General Alfred H. Terry. Their mission was to coerce the Lakota Sioux and the Cheyenne nations back to their allotted reservations. Despite the Hollywood versions of large Indian battles, the Indians very rarely fought large engagements against the U.S. cavalry, and the sight of a large force normally guaranteed their compliance and retreat back to their reservations.

However, after years of mistreatment and broken promises the Indian nations had had enough. Under Chief Sitting Bull and his war chief, Crazy Horse, the tribes were assembling in never-before-seen numbers, determined to strike a blow against the "long hairs," if only to regain some of their lost pride.

Terry's column was supported by two others already in the field, under General Crook and Colonel Gibbon, and over the next 4 weeks they criss-crossed the territory looking for the elusive tribes. On June 21 they received word from their scouts that "some Indians" were in the vicinity of the Little Bighorn River. Custer was instructed to proceed south along that stream in the hope that they could trap any Indians found between him and the other forces circling behind them. Impatient to get to any potential engagement first, Custer declined a Gatling gun battery, saying, "It will slow me down," and four additional cavalry companies, saying his force could handle anything it met.

On Saturday, June 24, several old Indian campsites were discovered, and Custer's Crow scouts reported to him that some Sioux were actually in the Little Bighorn valley. Believing the Indians would scatter when they saw him, Custer decided to strike immediately rather than wait for the other columns to arrive on June 26.

At noon on June 25, at the Rosebud and Little Bighorn River junction, Custer divided his troops. For a general who had been in charge of a balloon reconnaissance unit in the Civil War, Custer yet again paid little attention to scouting. Believing that the Indians had at most 1,300 warriors to oppose him, and that they would not make a stand against his cavalry, he rushed to action. The left column, under Major Reno, made its way down the riverbank, heading for a village the scouts had discovered some 2 miles away. Immediately Reno was confronted by a surprisingly large force of warriors, forcing him to dismount his troops and fight in a skirmish line on the edge of the surrounding timber forest. With ammunition dwindling and no sign of Custer, Reno and his command were forced to withdraw to the bluffs on the east of the river.

Custer meanwhile had found the battle he was desperate for. Believing the large dust cloud ahead of him was the retreating Indians he sought, he raced his column north, straight into more than 5,000 Sioux and Cheyenne warriors, eager for blood. The fight was short. The Indians swarmed over the Seventh, cutting them down as they fought desperately to escape. Even if he had not split his command, it is doubtful that many would have survived that day. The worst defeat ever sustained by the U.S. Army against Indians saw Custer die with 268 of his command, with another 60 in other skirmishes severely wounded.

Although pictures show Custer fighting to the end with his long blond locks flowing around him, he was in fact the only white man not scalped that day because he had had a crew cut a couple of days before, and wearing his trademark buckskins he was not even recognized by the Indians.

The tribes released all their pent-up anger in an extensive mutilation of the dead cavalry, stripping them and hacking them to pieces before finally retreating away from General Terry and his support columns and eventually making a permanent peace some 12 months later.

Had Custer held back from battle for one more day, it is doubtful there would have even been a fight, but yet again, his need for personal glory dictated his actions.

Interestingly, the Democratic nominations for the White House were to be held 3 days later, and he'd even brought his own reporter, Mark Kellogg, along with him. Had he defeated the Indian nations arraigned against him on June 26, there would still have been time to get a report of his victory back to Washington and help him realize the dream of the White House. Always surrounding himself with hangers-on and admirers, he took four other Custers, including his brother Tom, to their death that morning. The only survivor of the battle was a horse, ironically called Comanche, who was found in a thicket with seven arrows in his body.

MENUS

Although Custer was more than happy to serve hardtack to his men (flour and water softened in coffee to make it edible), his personal cook, Eliza Davidson, traveled everywhere with him to prepare his favorite dishes, even when he was in hard pursuit of the enemy.

Custer hunted every day and on one expedition bagged forty-one antelope, four buffalo, four elk, seven deer, two white wolves, and one red fox, along with "geese, ducks, prairie-chickens and sage-hens without number."

Last Meal

Roasted Buffalo Steaks

Beans and Molasses, Roasted Wild Corn

Prairie Hen

Texas-Style Game Hens (4)

½ cup apple jelly
½ cup ketchup
1 tbsp vinegar
½ tsp chili powder
½ tsp salt

½ tsp garlic powder
½ tsp chili powder
4 (1–1¼ lb) Cornish hens, split

- Combine the first 4 ingredients in a small saucepan and stir well. Cook over medium heat until the jelly melts, stirring constantly. Remove the sauce from the heat and keep warm.
- Combine salt, garlic powder, and chili powder, stirring well; sprinkle over the hens. Grill over medium coals for 45 minutes; turn occasionally. Baste with sauce. Grill an additional 15 minutes. Turn and baste frequently with remaining sauce. Let stand 10 to 15 minutes before slicing.

Roasted Wild Corn

- Strip the outer leaves back from the corn, leaving them still connected to the cob; remove the cornsilk and fold the leaves back over the corn.
- Place on a hot grill, or fire, for about 30 minutes.
- Peel off the leaves; smother with butter.

Venison, Moose, or Elk Steaks and Chops

If they are cut from young animals, they will need no marinating. The meat should hang for about 2 or 3 weeks and then be properly cut by your butcher.

- To cook the young steaks or chops, heat a heavy skillet until it's quite hot and then add butter and oil. Sauté the meat, turning it frequently to brown on all sides without charring. If you like, you can flame the meat with cognac just before serving. Steak and chops from young animals may be cooked in the same manner as beefsteaks or lamb chops, broiled, grilled, or sautéed. When broiling or cooking on an outdoor grill, cook quickly and do not overcook. Game will become tough or dry with long broiling or frying. Add salt and pepper at the end to taste.

Beef Jerky

A staple of the cavalry, when they had fresh meat and time to prepare it.

1 flank of London broil or other lean cut (e.g., buffalo or horse)
salt and pepper
1 cup soy sauce

- Cut the steak into thin strips; always cut with the grain of the meat.
- Dip the meat into the soy sauce. Lay the strips of meat out on a rack and sprinkle them with salt and pepper.
- Cook in 150°F oven for 10 hours.

Roast Buffalo Steaks

Bison meat is very low in fat and cholesterol; being very lean, it tends to cook much faster than beef, so watch the steaks carefully. Steaks can be ordered in any size, from 8 oz to 2 lb. When cooked on the grill they produce a delicious dish.

- Always use a low grill temperature.
- Flip the steaks with tongs; never use forks or puncture the meat because this lets the juices escape.
- Don't use salt during cooking; it dries up the meat. Instead, salt to taste after cooking.
- Never overcook buffalo; it's best served medium rare.

Beans and Molasses

- Open regular tins of baked beans. Add to a skillet with chunks of ham or bacon and about 1 pint of black molasses to every 3 lb beans.
- Let stew slowly for about 1 hour; serve hot.

ADOLF HITLER
The Führerbunker, Berlin, Germany
April 30, 1945

Soldiers of the Eastern Front! . . . Our mortal enemy, the Jewish Bolshevik, has begun his final massive attack. He hopes to smash Germany and wipe out our people. . . . If in the coming days and weeks every soldier on the Eastern Front does his duty, Asia's last assault will fail. . . . Berlin remains German, Vienna shall once more be German, and Europe shall never be Russian. . . . At this hour the entire German population looks to you, my fighters of the East, and hopes that through your tenacity, your fanaticism, by your weapons and under your leadership, the Bolshevik attack will drown in a bath of blood. At this very moment fate has removed the greatest war criminal of all time [President Franklin Roosevelt] from the world, the turning point of this war shall be determined.

—Adolf Hitler, April 13, 1945

Adolf Hitler's final master plan to "suck the Russians" into Berlin, thus relieving the pressure on his eastern armies, allowing them to regroup and attack the Russians from the rear, was greeted with silent groans from his general staff, who had already seen their mighty forces whittled away to practically nothing in the hands of this failed painter from upper Austria.

The "eastern forces" did not really exist, long dispersed or shivering in Russian gulags. Their "forces" consisted of old men, the wounded, and young boys from the Hitler Youth with guns thrust into their hands. The Third Reich was coming to its last days and all knew it, but no one could admit it and stand up to Adolf Hitler, the Führer.

How a lowly corporal who served in, and saw, the horrors of World War I could take a defeated people in his hands and inspire them to yet another conflict that would claim more than 50 million lives has to be one of the most incredible stories of all time.

Adolf Hitler was born in Braunau am Inn in Upper Austria, initially living a miserable existence as a third-rate artist. He enrolled in the Bavarian Infantry at the outbreak of World War I, earning two Iron Crosses. A background of rampant anti-Semitism after the war helped him to form an obscure German Workers' Party at the end of the hostilities, which later became the National Socialist German Workers' Party, or the Nazis. In politics he found an outlet for his vitriol and a vehicle for his ambitions that no one could have dreamed of.

Suddenly discovering within himself a power of demographic oratory in open air tirades in Munich against the Jews and the Treaty of Versailles, he cunningly tapped into the German resentment of the settlement terms from the war. This stirred their inborn sense of superiority over others, twisting all the blame for their problems onto the Jews and their partners, the victorious Allies.

Even 13 months in jail did not quell his hatred, and he used the time to write his successful book, *Mein Kampf*. His party began to grow rapidly, becoming the second most powerful political force in Germany. The world depression and rising unemployment elevated his status even more in the eyes of a desperate German people. President Hindenburg tried to keep him under control by making him chancellor in 1933, but within months he had died and Hitler had declared himself head of state, the Führer.

As the Allies looked on, he rearmed the new Germany at a rapid rate, creating a Berlin–Rome Axis with Mussolini in 1937. He suddenly annexed Austria, then overran Czechoslovakia in 1939, all the while keeping the Russians on the sidelines with the nonaggression pact on August 21. He then invaded Poland on September 1, which finally snapped the Allies out of their stupor and caused the declaration of World War II by the Allies on September 3, 1939.

Effortlessly sweeping through Denmark, Holland, and Norway, Hitler considered the war over when his German troops entered Paris on June 22, 1940, while the British troops simultaneously exited the continent at Dunkirk. Believing the British would stay holed up in England, he believed he could mop up the remains of Europe at his leisure.

This show of newfound German might brought the adulation of his people and the realization that their dream of a thousand-year reich might be possible after all.

And so with Europe in his hands, Hitler turned his attention to Germany's perennial foe, Russia. Finally invading on June 22, 1941, his armies besieged Stalingrad and even reached to within 25 miles of Moscow. But like Napoleon before him, he had not taken into account the long supply lines needed as the Russians retreated before him, adopting a scorched-earth policy as they went, destroying their own country to prevent succor for the Nazis. A worse foe than the Russians now struck: The Soviet winter arrived, freezing the panzer tanks and men alike. Bitter cold seized once smooth-running engines, and now the Russians, using Siberian and Cossack troops inured to the cold, launched their controlled counterattack that eventually took them to the gates of Berlin. Like Napoleon's, the bodies of Hitler's troops marked the long retreat. But the loss of so many only caused Hitler to fire his "incompetent" generals.

He now assumed control of the armies personally, but his inexperience was obvious and disaster followed disaster as his battered armies retreated from Russia, leaving 90,000 prisoners and many more thousands dead at Stalingrad alone.

With the Allied landing in Normandy on June 5–6, 1944, the writing was on the wall for Germany. Hitler's generals tried to plead with him to come to terms and then eventually tried to kill him themselves with a bomb. Neither tactic worked. Hitler was determined to fight on, a decision that took many more millions to the grave with him in the next 10 months.

On February 12, 1945, the State Department in Washington was convinced that Hitler and his staff, supported by some 200,000 elite troops, were preparing a last stand in the National Redoubt, built in heavily wooded mountains near Hitler's famous getaway, The Eagle's Nest.

Given this information, and believing the capture of Hitler was more important than the taking of Berlin, Allied commander General Dwight Eisenhower turned his attention to the coming assault on the Redoubt, leaving the Russians free to take Berlin.

It was only on April 23, when the captured German lieutenant general Kurt Dittmer said that all he knew of a fortress was something he had read in a Swiss newspaper the year before, that the Allies realized their mistake. Hitler was in Berlin and determined to remain there for his last stand.

An increasingly manic Hitler was ensconced in the Reich bunker, a concrete fortification built under the Reich Chancellery in the center of Berlin. With a concrete roof some 18 feet thick and walls 5 feet thick, the thirty rooms on two levels, though badly ventilated and cramped, were impervious to the heavy shelling that was reducing Berlin. Going upstairs to the Chancellery on April 20 to celebrate his 56th birthday with his 33-year-old girlfriend, Eva Braun, Hitler retained hope that the increasingly fractious relationship between Stalin's Russia and the other Allies would bring salvation for him and his people. The American–British alliance would surely side with him against the barbarians from the East, although it looked as if it would be at the last moment.

However, Hitler's fury at the "ineptness" of his generals grew daily in the confines of the Reich bunker. His mood swings were not helped by his doctor, who gave him large daily amphetamine injections, along with a mysterious cocaine-based eye drop for some unknown ailment that Hitler insisted on taking at doses more than five times the prescribed recommendation.

At his birthday party in the Chancellery, Hitler presented Iron Crosses to young boys before exhorting them to defend the Reich to the last and sending them out onto the streets to confront the fierce Russians, who were only blocks away. As Berlin was being flattened, his mistress, Eva Braun, played their only gramophone record over and over as they sipped champagne. The tune was called "Red Roses Bring You Happiness."

As the Russian stranglehold on the city tightened it was obvious to everyone that the end was near, but Hitler obstinately refused to take the last chance to flee Berlin, insisting that he would die with the city.

Finally, on April 28, seeing the end was nigh, he dictated his last will and testament to his secretary, Traudl Junge, who later described him as a "pleasant boss and a fatherly friend." In a simple ceremony he then married Eva Braun and, not trusting the cyanide capsule he was given, as he thought there was a plot to drug him and hand him over to the Russians, he gave it to his dog Blondi to see how effective it was. Seeing his dog expire quickly, he administered one to his new bride, then sitting in his office in front of the ever-present picture of his mother, he shot himself with a Walther pistol.

His physician, Dr. Stumpfegger, helped carry the couple up the four flights of stairs to the garden of the Chancellery, laying Eva's body on Hitler's right and then drenching them with gasoline and burning them to a crisp.

As the great war finally came to an end, three of the world's leaders of the mighty conflict perished within 19 days of each other: Mussolini at the hands of his own people, Roosevelt by the hand of God, and Hitler, who started it all, by his own hand.

MENUS

In September 1931 Hitler became vegetarian after the suicide of his niece Geli Raubal, whom he loved (she shot herself), but he was often caught eating meat, especially his favorite liver dumplings.

Last Meal

Vegetable Soup and Mashed Potatoes

Favorite Dinner Dishes

Roasted Squab

Pan-Fried Trout

Sautéed Potatoes

Liver Dumplings

Onion Pie

His personal chef for many years was Marlene Kunda, who made great nonmeat food, until he discovered she was a Jew, whereupon she disappeared from history.

Favorites

Chocolates (2 lb a day) and Pastries

Hot Chocolate with Whipped Cream

Sugar

He always took seven spoons of sugar in his tea and even added spoonfuls of sugar to his wine.

Hitler's Vegetable Soup

Hitler liked his soup thick and creamy, prepared by his dietitian, Marlene Von Exner, from 1943. She secretly added marrow fats to his meals because she despised his vegetarian diet.

½ cup onions
½ cup celery
½ cup chopped apple
1 cup potatoes
½ cup carrots
½ cup turnips
4 oz nut compound
1 apple sliced
1 cup flour
2 pints water
salt and pepper to taste

- Lightly poach the vegetables until soft. Remove from water and stir in the flour slowly until a soft roux is formed.
- Add the chopped apple and the nut compound and blend all the ingredients together gently.
- Purée, season to taste, thin if necessary with double cream, and serve garnished with sliced apples.

Roasted Squab

Dione Lucas, a chef in Hamburg, says he loved squab prepared this way.

6 tbsp or ¾ stick unsalted butter
4 squabs, ¾ to 1 lb each
20 juniper berries
salt and pepper to taste
4 slices brioche, at least ¾ inch thick

- Melt 4 tbsp butter in Dutch oven over medium heat. Add the birds and brown on all sides.
- Cover and cook over low heat until the breasts are medium rare (20 to 25 minutes), basting often.
- Crush the juniper berries with anything heavy.
- When the birds are about done, add the berries to the pan and season to taste. Cook over high heat for a few seconds, turning the squabs continuously.
- Melt the remaining butter and fry the bread until golden on each side.
- Serve.

Pan-Fried Trout (4)

4 rainbow trout, filleted
2 tbsp lemon juice
1 tsp salt
1 dash white pepper
1 dash Worcestershire sauce
flour as needed
2 tbsp butter

- Place the trout fillets in a glass dish; add lemon juice, salt, pepper, and Worcestershire sauce.
- Let stand for 5 minutes. Remove fillets, coat with flour.
- Place butter in 12-inch sauté pan; heat gently. Add fillets, skin side up. Sauté until golden, turn, and bake at 325°F for about 10 minutes.

Liver Dumplings (Lebeknoedel) (4)

1 lb ground liver
½ lb ground lean pork
1 cup breadcrumbs
1 cup bread soaked in water and pressed dry
1 egg
a little corn flour
¼ tsp grated nutmeg
1 minced onion
2 oz chopped fresh parsley
4 tsp butter
½ cup dry breadcrumbs

- Mix ingredients in order given except breadcrumbs and drop by the teaspoonful into boiling salted water. Boil for 15 minutes.
- Remove to serving dish and top with breadcrumbs, browned in butter.
- Serve with sauerkraut.

Onion Pie (Zwiebelkuchen) (8)

1 pack yeast, active dry
1 tsp sugar
1½ tsp salt
3 cups unbleached flour
1 tbsp shortening
1 cup water, 120°F to 130°F
6 bacon slices, cut up
2 medium onions, sliced
¼ tsp cumin
pepper as desired
1 egg yolk
1 cup sour cream

- Mix yeast, sugar, 1 tsp salt, and ½ cup flour.
- Blend in shortening and warm water; beat for 2 minutes.
- Add enough flour to make a soft dough. Knead dough until smooth and elastic, about 5 minutes.
- Place dough in a lightly greased bowl. Cover and let dough rise in a warm place for ½ hour. Pat dough into a lightly greased 12-inch pizza pan or onto a lightly greased baking sheet. Press up edges to make a slight rim.
- Fry bacon until crisp. Remove from grease and drain on absorbent paper.
- Add onions to bacon grease; cook slowly until tender but not brown.
- Sprinkle onion, bacon, cumin, ½ tsp salt, and pepper over dough.
- Bake at 400°F for 20 minutes.
- Blend egg yolk and sour cream. Pour over onions.
- Bake for 10 to 15 minutes longer or until golden brown and sour cream is set.
- Serve warm or at room temperature.

Sautéed Potatoes

2 lb peeled golden potatoes
3 tbsp olive oil

- Slice the potatoes in ¼-inch slices.
- Lightly boil the potatoes for about 6 minutes.
- Finish in sauté pan with oil until golden brown on both sides.

MARILYN MONROE
Brentwood, California
August 5, 1962

I knew I belonged to the public and to the world,
not because I was talented or beautiful, but because
I have never belonged to anything or anyone else.

—Marilyn Monroe

Born into poverty as Norma Jean Mortenson on June 1, 1926, the daughter of a mentally ill mother and a father she never knew, Marilyn Monroe nonetheless lived an incredibly eventful life, one that saw her become the most famous movie star on the planet. She was married to the world's greatest athlete, and then the greatest playwright, and eventually became the mistress of the world's most powerful man, all within a few short years.

Because social workers were forced to take her away from her mother at the age of 9 and she was put into her first orphanage, no one could have envisaged the career this determined little girl was about to embark on. Living with various foster parents through the 1930s, she always harbored the same dream, like so many California girls, of becoming a star in nearby Hollywood.

From an early age she realized the power she had over men, and in 1942, at the age of only 17, she married neighbor James Dougherty, the first of a series of tortured relationships with men. This became her longest affair and lasted until September 13, 1946, by which time she had decided that "Norma Jean" was not going to open the gates of Hollywood for her, so she changed her name to Marilyn Monroe.

Working as a cocktail waitress around movie lots, she used her sexuality to gain access to meetings with the movers and shakers at 20th Century Fox, and gradually her walk-on roles and bit parts became even bigger, particularly after she had a torrid affair with Stavros, the main financial power behind the studio itself.

French movie actor Yves Montand entered her life next, blatantly trying to use the up-and-coming starlet to position himself in the American movie industry.

"The World's Greatest Athlete," baseball legend Joe DiMaggio, then walked down the aisle with her in January 1953, but the divorce went through less than 18 months later as Marilyn, determined to make it to the top, would not allow him to pull her away from what he considered the evil decadence of Hollywood. However, DiMaggio's feelings for her were the most sincere. Of all the men in her life, he was the only one to attend her funeral years later. He had truly loved her.

Playwright Arthur Miller became her next husband in June 1956, and another turbulent relationship ebbed and flowed for the next 4 years. Yet again, Marilyn's obsessions with her movie career and deep distrust of men placed intolerable pressures on the marriage, causing yet another breakdown.

When a fling with Frank Sinatra failed as he left her for dancer Juliet Prowse, Marilyn entered the last years of her life in 1962 at her new home on Fifth Helena Drive. Finally at the top of her profession as a movie star, she was firmly in the sights of the world's most powerful man, John F. Kennedy, the president of the United States.

From childhood Marilyn had lived in almost forty different homes and had toured many Hollywood palaces looking for a special place where she could retreat from the world before falling in love with her humble home in Brentwood. There, surrounded by its high wall and privacy, she could retreat from the demands made on her by an ever more aggressive press and movie studio. Looked after by her housekeeper, Eunice Murray, Marilyn often disappeared for days into her own private world, using the phone as her contact with the outside before sweeping into the studio to film her latest picture, *Something's Got to Give*, with her co-star, Dean Martin, a movie widely tipped to be a blockbuster.

Marilyn's routine was always the same, spending hours on the phone in the evening, sipping her favorite drink, Dom Perignon 1953, before slipping on a bra, earmuffs, and eye patches and settling down to sleep in her dark, heavily draped bedroom.

However, earlier that year she had caught the eye of President Kennedy, a man lauded at the time for his perfect marriage and the new sense of dignity and morality he had brought to the White House. Many years later the illusion was shattered, and he was revealed as a lothario who had nude swimming pool parties in the White House, raucous cocktail parties on Air Force One, and a marriage of convenience with wife Jackie Kennedy, who was reportedly paid $1 million by his father, Joe, to stay with him and create the illusion of "Camelot," the promised land. The man who built the walls around him and hid the potential scandals from the public was his brother Bobby, who often used the full power of his position as attorney general to bury incriminating documents and details of all the Kennedy indiscretions, particularly his own, for decades.

Long-distance flirting on the phone with Marilyn by the president turned into a clandestine affair in which she would often appear at his secret penthouse in New York on 57th Street.

With a major convention coming up in Madison Square Garden, the president had cajoled Marilyn for weeks to sing "Happy Birthday" to him at the end of the conference, despite the frantic urgings of his own staff to distance himself from this obvious liability.

Marilyn accepted and had a special see-through gown prepared, and she often shocked everyone on the set of her movie by frequently calling JFK on his personal number at all times of the day and night in front of any number of people. The popular press of the day refused to believe that their perfect president could be involved in anything untoward, and they ignored the obvious signs of what would have been the scoop of the century.

Hearing that Marilyn was coming to New York for the event, Jackie Kennedy gave JFK an ultimatum: "If she comes, I don't." Jackie spent the weekend horseback riding in Virginia.

Seeing their movie and its budget come under pressure as Marilyn drove full tilt into her "secret" relationship, the executives at Fox demanded she not go to New York, saying if she did she would be in breach of contract and would be fired.

A worried Marilyn called JFK, and he said, "Don't worry, Bobby will fix it." Within hours his brother, the attorney general of the United States, was on the phone to Fox executives to elicit the release of their sex symbol for a 2-minute song for the president 3,000 miles away.

Believing the matter had been dealt with, Marilyn went to New York on May 17 and stunned the nation by singing "Happy Birthday" in a breathless voice, wearing the specially designed see-through dress. The president couldn't keep his eyes, and later his hands, off her at his 57th Street hideaway, where she met his brother Bobby for the first time. This was their last time together, however; on returning to the Fox studios, Marilyn found that her private access number to JFK was greeted with a "disconnected" message, and no amount of screaming at the White House switchboard could get her put through. Yet again, another man had turned his back on her.

The Kennedys' brother-in-law, Peter Lawford, lived near Marilyn, and she quickly turned to him for help in finding out why she had been shunted aside. Receiving little help from Lawford, she turned to "Mr. Fix-It," as Bobby was called, knowing he had been instructed by the president to get rid of her, because JFK was now fixated on Mafia call girl Judith Exner. Bobby's attempts to placate Marilyn led to a torrid affair between them as Marilyn found the intellectual charms of Bobby even more attractive than the brother who had so cruelly dumped her.

Once again, thinking she'd found love, Marilyn told anyone who wanted to listen about her newfound happiness. And once again she was devastated as Bobby, under the instructions of his mother, Rose Kennedy, was told to clean up his act and support his brother Teddy, who was running for senator in Massachusetts. Bobby Kennedy quickly disappeared from her world with all the coldness of his brother. Yet again the private phone number she had been given to his desk in the Justice Department answered, "You have reached a nonworking number at the Justice Department. Please hang up and try again."

This was the last straw for Marilyn. Realizing how the brothers had used her, she was incandescent with rage. She really believed that Bobby loved her, not realizing that with the Kennedy family, politics was their only mistress. Repeated attempts to get him to confront her face to face, if only just to end it, failed as the power of the U.S. government erected a wall of silence around both brothers.

On Saturday, August 4, 1962, Bobby finally agreed to see her, and with Peter Lawford he took a helicopter to the Fox lot in Hollywood and drove to her home in Brentwood, where she had a Mexican buffet prepared for their meeting.

Marilyn got no warmth from the now stony attorney general, and as he left she was already calling her publicist to arrange a press conference for Monday morning, when she would "finally reveal the dirt on the Kennedy brothers," a meeting she would never attend.

At 5 A.M. the next morning the Los Angeles police were notified that Marilyn Monroe had been found dead. Rushing to the house, they were eventually informed by Eunice Murray and analyst Ralph Greenson that Marilyn had died around midnight.

The nude Marilyn, with her arms by her side and legs perfectly straight, was lying face-down on her bed with the lights on, something she never did. When police asked about the delay in calling them, Greenson said, "We had to call the studio publicity department first."

Interestingly, all her personal files were gone from the house, and the police noted that Murray was calmly doing her third load of laundry in the laundry room at 5 A.M. A hasty autopsy showed Marilyn had died from an overdose, but later tests revealed that her kidneys were untouched by the huge amount of drugs she would have had to consume. Her telephone records for the previous days had disappeared; according to the telephone company, "men in black suits with shiny shoes" had taken them.

Marilyn Monroe died at the age of 36. She'd entered the world denied by one man, her father, and exited it deserted by another.

MENUS

As Marilyn tried to woo back Bobby Kennedy on the night of her death, she had a Mexican buffet delivered to her Brentwood home.

Gazpacho

6 large ripe tomatoes
4 large cucumbers
2 large green peppers
8 spring onions
4 cloves garlic
2 tsp salt
⅔ cup olive oil
½ cup red wine vinegar
36 oz tomato juice
1 cup water
4 tbsp Worcestershire sauce
pepper to taste

- Blanch and peel tomatoes; chop fine with the cucumber, green peppers, and spring onions.
- Chop the garlic, add to the vinegar and oil, and whisk together.
- Add all the other ingredients and chill overnight.

Mexican Peacocks

This unusual and delicious recipe is always a hit. It's a great way to introduce your family to Mexican cuisine. You must start this recipe early in the day to let the coating on the chicken chill and set.

4 boneless, skinless chicken breasts
1 large ripe avocado
¼ cup butter
2 garlic cloves, minced
¼ cup flour
¼ cup milk
1 egg, beaten
1 to 1½ cups dried breadcrumbs
oil for frying

- Place the chicken breasts between two sheets of waxed paper and gently pound until they are ¼ inch thick. Be careful not to make holes or weak spots in the chicken.
- Mash together the avocado, butter, and garlic and place 2 tbsp in the center of each flattened chicken breast. Fold the chicken over to enclose stuffing. Dust the filled chicken bundles with flour, then dip in milk. Drain, then dip in beaten egg, then into the crumbs. Dip again into egg, then again into crumbs. This part gets messy, but it's crucial that the chicken be thickly coated with breadcrumbs. Chill in the refrigerator for 5 to 6 hours.
- Place enough oil in a heavy skillet to reach ½ inch thickness. Fry chicken in oil until golden on each side, about 3 to 4 minutes. Remove.

Layered Taco Dip

This wonderful, colorful dip is very popular and really looks beautiful. It became widely known in the 1980s. When you spread the different dips on the platter, make each new layer slightly smaller than the one beneath, so all the different colors and textures show. Substitute your favorite refrigerated dips for any of the layers to make it even easier.

    1 can refried beans
    1 cup salsa
    2 cups sour cream
    2 avocados
    2 tbsp lime juice or lemon juice
    1 clove garlic, minced
    2 tbsp sour cream
    1 cup salsa
    2 cups shredded lettuce
    2 tomatoes, seeded and chopped
    2 cups pepper jack cheese
    olives if desired
    tortilla chips

- In a medium bowl, mix beans and 1 cup salsa and spread evenly on a 12-inch round platter. Top with 2 cups sour cream.
- Mash avocados with lime juice, garlic, and 2 tbsp sour cream. Spread over sour cream on platter.
- Top with remaining 1 cup salsa.
- Sprinkle with lettuce, then tomatoes and cheese.
- Refrigerate 2 hours to blend flavors, then serve with tortilla chips and vegetables.

Mexican Meatballs (4)

1 lb lean ground beef
¼ cup white cornmeal
1 egg, lightly beaten
1 clove garlic
1 small onion, minced
½ tsp dried oregano, crumbled
1 tsp salt
½ tsp ground black pepper

Sauce:
1 tbsp butter or margarine
1 small onion, chopped
1 clove garlic
2 tbsp chili powder
½ tsp ground cumin
¼ tsp dried oregano, crumbled
3 cups tomato juice
salt to taste

- Mix meatball ingredients together; shape into small balls about ½ inch in diameter.
- In a large saucepan, melt butter or margarine. Add chopped onion and cook slowly until lightly browned. Add garlic, chili powder, cumin, oregano, tomato juice, and salt to taste. Bring to a boil. Drop meatballs into boiling sauce, cover, and simmer for about 10 minutes or until meatballs are cooked.

Refried Beans

Use to fill tortillas, adding grated cheese, chopped fresh vegetables, and salsa to taste.

    2–3 tbsp olive oil
    1 tsp ground coriander
    2 onions, chopped
    chili powder to taste
    4 cloves garlic, crushed
    18 oz cooked red kidney beans
    1 tsp ground cumin

- Heat the oil and add the onion, garlic, cumin, coriander, and chili if used.
- Stir fry 2 minutes.
- Add the beans and stir until everything is heated through. Mash some of the beans if you wish.

Veal Parmigiana (4)

2 lb veal, thinly sliced
1 cup flavored breadcrumbs
1 lb beefsteak mozzarella, thinly sliced
3 cups pints tomato sauce
2 eggs
¼ cup milk

- Mix milk and eggs in a bowl. Dip each piece of veal into the milk and eggs, then cover with breadcrumbs.
- In frying pan, fry each piece gently on both sides.
- Then put in a pan about 9 inches × 13 inches × 2 inches.
- Put slices of cheese and a spoonful of tomato sauce on each piece.
- Bake at 350°F until cheese is melted, about 15 minutes.

CAPTAIN JAMES COOK
Kealakekua Bay, Hawaii
February 14, 1779

Thus fell our great and excellent commander.

—Lieutenant King's diaries

Born in Marton in the County of Yorkshire, England, on October 27, 1728, James Cook became one of history's greatest explorers, from the most unlikely background. The son of a farm laborer and part of a system that condemned the poor to leave school at age 12 and work as adults in the mines, he displayed enormous drive and courage to teach himself to become a master navigator, sailor, and global adventurer.

Like those of so many other great figures in history, his public achievements seemed to be mirrored by deep personal tragedy. Four of his siblings died in infancy, and a fifth by the age of 23. All his children died before him, and two of them died without ever seeing his face. For a sea captain it was especially traumatic that his first two sons, James and Nathaniel, both drowned, unable to swim.

Merry England in the 1750s saw boys become men quickly, as war with Napoleon's France had the Royal Navy enlisting children as young as 10 years old to help crew its ships. Cook's ability to absorb lessons quickly and his inquiring mind ensured his rapid promotion through the ranks, and he quickly became a ship's master at an early age.

He discovered innate mathematical skills within himself, and this, coupled with his compassionate treatment of his men, immediately marked him out as a future captain, highly regarded by his superiors.

Drafted to Nova Scotia on the *Pembroke* to fight the French in Canada, he became appalled at the high mortality rate among the crews. Like another great sailor of his generation, Admiral Nelson, he realized that many of these deaths could be avoided by very simple methods. After losing almost half his crew in less than 6 months, he vowed that the old methods were finished. Fresh fruits and vegetables were literally forced on his men along with high standards of hygiene and cleanliness. Other captains started to copy his example, and service in the Royal Navy became a career, not a death sentence.

While he served in Canada, his accurate charting of the St. Lawrence River made the amphibious assault by the British on Quebec possible, eventually leading to the collapse of the French domination in Canada.

Returning to England for a 1-year break in 1762, he married Elizabeth Batts, some 13 years his junior. Like many other seafarers' wives, she realized only too late that her husband's first love was the sea. She could never have imagined her lot being to bear him a string of children, and then to inform him of their deaths when he returned from some voyage 2 or 3 years later.

On August 1, 1768, he took command of the *Endeavour* and sailed into history in New Zealand, where he began to produce incredibly accurate charts of the newly discovered country, setting the standard for the world's finest nautical maps by the Royal Navy.

In the next 2 years he charted the coast of Queensland, Australia, and though originally naming his discoveries South Wales and Stingray Harbour, he eventually changed their names to New South Wales and Botany Bay.

Returning to a hero's welcome in England after nearly 3 years' absence from a journey that covered 30,000 miles and saw him chart more than 5,000 miles of new coastline, he was greeted with the news that his third son, Joseph, had died after only 1 month of life. Picking up the pieces of his marriage at home in Whitby, he was present when his fourth son, George, mysteriously died on July 8, 1772.

For a man who lavished so much care and attention on his crews and their well-being, he seems to have been curiously detached from the feelings of his young bride. Five days after George's death, now in command of the *Resolution* and its sister ship *Adventure*, he set out on his second great voyage of discovery. In January 1773 he became the first sailor to cross the Antarctic line and the first to circumnavigate the globe in both directions.

For many centuries there had always been rumors of a great southern continent, but by Cook's third crossing of the Antarctic Circle he was able to prove that all that existed was an icy wasteland with no possible material use to the Crown.

Although he was bitterly disappointed at not being able to find more territory for the empire, his voyage was lauded for the new techniques he used to promote the health of his ships' crews. Only one man out of 118 succumbed to disease, an unheard of statistic for the day.

Cook was received in England by King George III as a national hero on July 30, 1775, after another 3 long years at sea. Cook's enthusiasm at being reunited with his wife immediately led to another pregnancy for her and the birth of his fifth son, Hugh, who was born on May 25, 1977. But only 10 months after his return, Cook was already provisioning the ships *Resolution* and *Discovery* for his last great voyage, which began on July 12, 1776, only 18 days after Hugh's birth.

The mission was to find the fabled Northwest Passage that would supposedly open up the entire American continent. Sailing down the coast of Africa, he rounded the Cape of Good Hope, crossed the Indian Ocean, and bypassed New Zealand, Tasmania, and the Friendly Islands, where the not-so-friendly natives tried to kill him as he put in for water.

On January 18, 1778, he discovered a new chain of islands that he named the Sandwich Islands after one of his sponsors, the Earl of Sandwich. These were later renamed Hawaii.

Continuing to Oregon still looking for the elusive passage, he now discovered the territory of Alaska and charted Anchorage Bay before heading into the Bering Straits, where he was turned back by heavy ice.

Deciding to wait out the winter in the Pacific, he discovered the island of Maui, where his best officer, William Bligh (later to command the infamous *Bounty*), produced superb charts of the coastline. His charts were setting a standard for other navies to emulate.

After another 2 months he decided to move on yet again and finally found a safe anchorage at Kealakekua Bay on the Kiona coast of the big island.

For many of his years at sea fortune had always seemed to favor Cook, enabling him to record many achievements, and once again his fabled luck seemed to be in. As he entered the bay on January 16, 1779, the natives had just begun the Makahiki festival, a period of great feasting dedicated to the fertility god Lono.

Sexual partners were usually exchanged and all rules were suspended as the smell of Hawaiian pit roasts and feasting hung over the bay for almost a month to celebrate the legend of the god Lono.

The Hawaiians believed their god Lono, who was represented by a small wooden figure perched on a tall mastlike crossbeam on which were hung long white sheets of taro leaves, would one day return to them. Kealakekua Bay was the ancestral home of the god, and as Cook arrived with his ships and their tall masts and large sails, who else could be arriving but Lono himself?

Captain Cook and his crew were treated like gods for nearly a month; the ships were fully provisioned with timber, wild pigs, and the freshest fruits and vegetables. The native women threw themselves at the sailors, many of whom had not seen a woman for years.

The Hawaiians had no interest in gold or beads; the islanders coveted only nails and other simple metal objects. Women gave themselves to the sailors for any simple piece of metal.

Cook further enhanced his god status by amazing the natives with a firework display. It both shocked and terrified the

Hawaiians, who had no concept of gunpowder and were over-awed by the powers of these strangers.

However, Cook's luck was beginning to change. With little warning one of his crew, William Watman, died of a stroke, showing the superstitious natives that maybe these were only mortal men after all.

As relations rapidly became strained, Cook and his crew got the message that their time was up and sailed away on February 4, 1779, straight into the mouth of a fearsome Pacific storm.

After fighting heavy seas for more than a week, the battered ships were forced to return to Kealakekua Bay, which, with the end of the festival, they found deserted except for a few fishers. Word soon got around that the god Lono had been battered in his own domain, and the natives flocked to the bay to see the Englishmen struggle to repair their tattered vessels.

James Cook then made one of his few mistakes. Reacting to the theft of one of his small boats by some islanders, he sought to take King Kalaniopau hostage in exchange for the return of his cutter. This infuriated the Hawaiians, who had already given him everything they had, from women to food, receiving in return only a few nails, a violin, and sexually transmitted diseases.

As the king sat on the beach, encouraged by his wife not to trust these "haoles," his warriors got more and more enraged. Then word came that some marines had shot and killed a lesser chief, Nookemai, for attempting to leave the bay in a canoe.

This was the last straw. One warrior advanced on Cook and struck him with his heavy wooden club. Cook fell. "Lono" was mortal. Immediately the marines with him were attacked, and although they tried to fire volleys, they were slowly forced to re-treat to their boats, leaving Cook knee deep in water, facing the native charge alone, with the bodies of four marines floating around him. The soldiers flung themselves into the ocean and swam for their lives to the boats waiting offshore. Cook could not follow his soldiers to safety because, like his sons before, he couldn't swim.

The natives stripped the dead captain but refrained from eating him, as was their normal custom. Later they returned some of his bones and both hands, preserved in salt, to the shaken crews of his ships.

His remains were put in a coffin. With great fanfare, his grieving crew buried James Cook in the waters of the bay on February 21, 1779.

MENUS

When King Kamehameha III had a banquet for 10,000 of his subjects in true Hawaiian style in 1847, they cooked for more than 12,000—and ate it all.

Some of the Items Consumed

271 Hogs

482 Calabashes of Poi

602 Chickens

12 Oxen

Salt Pork

12 Barrels of Lai Lai

Cabbages, Onions

Bananas, Pineapples, Coconuts, Oranges, Limes, Grapes

4,000 Heads of Taro

180 Large Squid

When Cook arrived in Kealakekua Bay, the festival that greeted him went on for almost a month.

Some of the Dishes Presented to Cook

Kalua pig can be prepared with either a whole pig (any size) or a smaller piece of pork roast. I enclose both recipes but strongly recommend the whole pig method for a large gathering.

Kalua Pig I

1 whole pig
banana leaves
salt and pepper
lemons
garlic

- The night before, dig a pit in the ground away from any building to a depth of about 2 feet.
- Find lava rock or large porous rocks about 1–2 lb in weight and any cuts of hardwood (e.g., eucalyptus, oak).
- Put a layer of stones on the bottom of the pit and build a fire with the wood and some more rocks (for the pig cavity).
- After 4 to 5 hours the fire should be burned to ashes.
- Take the pig and rub hard inside and out with salt and pepper, lemons, and garlic.
- Using tongs take some of the red-hot rocks and place in the cavity of the pig, then tie the legs together.
- Rake the ashes from the fire and store in a heatproof tub.
- Cover the surface with banana leaves and lower the pig (preferably in a wire basket) onto the fire pit.
- Surround it with heavy-duty aluminum foil, cover with more banana leaves, then heap back the hot rocks and ashes over the pig. Cover completely; don't leave any holes.
- Sprinkle with water and roast for about 5 more hours. Pork should be dropping off the bones by this time.
- Serve with Hawaiian poi and sea salt.

Kalua Pig II (8)

6 lb pork butt roast
5 cups water
3 tsp liquid smoke
¼ cup Hawaiian rock salt

- Place pork in a roasting tray.
- Mix together liquid smoke, rock salt, and water. Pour over the pork. Cover with aluminum foil and cook at 400°F for 3 to 3½ hours.
- Remove pork from pan and shred.
- Serve with poi.

Poi

Poi is an extremely nutritious side dish made from the steamed and mashed taro plant.

- Peel the taro root, steam, and mash, adding a little water until it has a pudding-like texture. Chill and serve within a day.

Lobos Poke (8)

3 lb fresh tuna or other firm fish
1 finely chopped onion
6 thinly sliced spring onions
1 tbsp freshly grated ginger
2 chili peppers (Hawaiian if possible), seeded and chopped
1 tbsp sesame oil
Hawaiian salt to taste
2 tsp toasted sesame seeds

- Cut fish into cubes about 1 inch square and in a large bowl combine all the ingredients except for the sesame seeds.
- Chill for about 6 hours; sprinkle the sesame on top and serve.

Chicken Long Rice (8)

6 lb chicken thighs
4 slices of crushed fresh ginger
1 packet long rice
6 minced green onions
4 pinches rock salt

- Soak rice in water to soften.
- Put chicken in a large pot and cover with water and ginger. Bring to a boil. Simmer for 45 minutes to an hour, until the chicken meat falls off the bones.
- Strain the broth, throw out the bones, and put the chicken meat back in the broth.
- Add the long rice and simmer until the rice has absorbed about half the liquid in the pot.
- Serve garnished with green onions and rock salt.

Haupia (Coconut Milk Dessert) (8)

3 cans coconut
5 cups milk
½ cup cornstarch
½ cup cane sugar

- Put aside ½ cup of the coconut.
- Heat milk gently and pour over the remaining coconut in a bowl and let stand for 45 minutes.
- Strain through a muslin cloth until all the liquid has gone through. Discard coconut.
- In a small pan blend the cornstarch and sugar; stir in the strained milk. Cook on low until it thickens, stirring constantly.
- Pour into a greased baking dish, sprinkle with remaining coconut, chill, cut, and serve.

JOHN FRANKLIN CANDY
Durango, Mexico
March 4, 1994

I think I became an actor to hide from myself.

—John Candy

One of the most beloved comics of our times, John Candy played the lovable, big-hearted buffoon in numerous movies in the 1980s and 1990s. Born in Toronto, Canada, on October 31, 1950, he rose to fame (after an average scholastic career that included studying for a journalism degree) as a member of the Toronto branch of the cult series *Second City Television* at the age of 27. He found a passion for acting while attending a local community college, which quickly led him to bit parts on various Canadian TV shows where talent, not looks, was the main requisite for employment.

John was overweight even as a child and received early warnings of future health problems because both his grandfather and his father died of heart attacks at an early age. His father, Sidney, died at the young age of 35, leaving his 5-year-old son to hide his grief with food, and later humor.

Second City Television became such an instant success that the NBC television network picked it up in 1981. John quickly brought his fantastic mimicry talents to the attention of Hollywood with a host of brilliant impersonations of people such as Orson Welles, Richard Burton, Don Rickles, Jackie Gleason, Luciano Pavarotti, Tom Selleck, Ed Asner, and many others. He also created a group of hilarious characters such as the handsome but inept TV actor Steve Roman, the hapless children's entertainer Mr. Messenger, smut merchant "Harry, the guy with a snake on his face," and his most popular, the unscrupulous street-beat TV personality Johnny LaRue. So popular did he become that many of his previously ignored Canadian films such as *The Clown Murders* became hot properties on the video circuit, ensuring the fledgling star a steady income.

His acting career took off in the early 1980s with appearances in movies such as *Splash*, *Stripes*, *Going Berserk*, *National Lampoon's Vacation*, and *The Blues Brothers*. John delivered a particularly great performance as Del Griffith in the comedy *Planes, Trains and Automobiles* and then popped up in a cameo on Ray Parker Jr.'s "Ghostbusters" video. His face was everywhere, and one of his main attributes was that he always appeared to be a regular guy, seemingly comfortable with his ballooning weight, which actually made him stand out alongside the slim, chiseled Hollywood stars he played alongside. His range of talent was such that he could make people laugh with a lift of an eyebrow. John never cared about being the headliner, often playing bit parts that didn't really do his talent justice and preferring to work with his close friends such as Rick Moranis.

In the late 1980s his weight gain became a cause of real concern to his friends and his wife, Rosemary, who had a boy named Christopher and a daughter named Jennifer with him. In the early 1990s he was almost unrecognizable from the man of only a decade earlier. At 6 feet 2 inches tall and always over 300 pounds, he was a big man in every way.

Never forgetting his Canadian roots, he used his movie money to become an owner of the Canadian Argonauts football team with Bruce McNall and hockey legend Wayne Gretzky. He never had a bad word to say about anyone and was loved by the public, who quickly realized that this big shambling bear of a man was in real life pretty much the character they loved on screen. Although he had made his name as a comic, as the 1980s waned he turned to play more serious roles, showing he was more than a one-trick pony. In 1991 he appeared in a romance called *Only the Lonely*, and later that year he excelled as a shady southern lawyer in Oliver Stone's *JFK*. Although his career often suffered dry spells, John never moped and always bounced back from any setback with the same good humor and grace he showed on screen. Even in the smallest roles he continued to show his genius, performing the voice of a talking horse in *Hot to Trot*, a weird disc jockey in *Little Shop of Horrors*, and a state trooper in the Sesame Street film *Follow That Bird*.

There was something so naturally funny about seeing him crammed into a police uniform that he was assigned that role in more than ten movies. He then hit a rocky patch with a string of commercial flops such as *Nothing but Trouble, Once upon a Crime*, and *Rookie of the Year*. When he saw that he was not doing himself justice, he descended into a downward spiral of excessive eating, drinking, and smoking. With his weight heading toward 350 pounds, and becoming increasingly aware of his genetic heritage, John tried to stop smoking and control his size, but this larger-than-life man had a larger-than-life appetite, and he found himself shedding a few pounds only to see them come back with interest.

He gave his greatest performance as a disgraced Olympic star in *Cool Runnings*, which seemed to point to a new path for him. With this upsurge in his career, John headed to Durango, Mexico, to film *Wagons East*, a movie that he had told his family would be his last because he'd spent only 3 weeks with them in the previous year. However, he also told Maureen O'Hara that he dreaded going there because the heat would kill him. Located about 100 miles northwest of Mexico City, with a constant temperature of well over 90°F, this location was not well suited to John. Staying in a room at the Camino Del Perque resort and paying some $3,000 a month, John vowed to get healthier and even brought his own chef with him, but the chef cooked more double cheeseburgers than salads, and nothing really changed. His troubles increased when the crew could not find a horse to carry him, and much of the movie became a series of body shots with a lighter actor filling in for him.

On March 3, 1994, John shot a series of exhausting action shots in the oppressive heat, with the shoot wrapping up about 10 P.M. John retired to his room and ordered a spaghetti meal, safe in the knowledge that with only two more scenes he could wrap up his final movie and be with his family forever. He ate his meal alone, then told his bodyguard, Gustavo Populus, that he would take a shower and go to bed. The next morning around 8 A.M., Populus called the villa, but there was no reply, and 15 minutes later he let himself in, finding his employer dead in a long black and red night-shirt. There were no signs of drugs, alcohol, or foul play, and the doctor quickly declared it "death from a massive heart attack." His wife mysteriously objected to any autopsy, and his body remained in the bed until 4 P.M., when they found four men strong enough to carry him to the ambulance.

He was buried on March 9 at St. Martin's Church in Brentwood, California, interestingly also Nicole Brown Simpson's church. Good friend Dan Aykroyd delivered the eulogy along with Rick Moranis, Bill Murray, Martin Short, Rhea Perlman, and a host of his peers. He was finally interred at the Holy Cross Cemetery in Culver City, two spaces above Fred MacMurray.

MENU

Mexican Spaghetti (4)

12 oz extra lean beef or turkey
1 finely chopped onion
1 cup chunky salsa
1 cup canned corn
¼ cup water
Salt and pepper, to taste
8 oz regular spaghetti
½ cup grated Monterey Jack cheese

- Cook beef and onion in large skillet, stirring frequently until brown. Stir in salsa, corn, water, and salt and pepper; cook until thickened.
- Prepare pasta according to package instructions, drain, toss warm pasta with sauce, and sprinkle with the cheese.